Racism and Black Resistance in Britain

RACISM AND

Robert Moore

BLACK RESISTANCE

in Britain

Pluto  Press

First published 1975 by Pluto Press Limited
Unit 10 Spencer Court, 7 Chalcot Road, London NW1 8LH
Copyright © Pluto Press 1975

ISBN 0 902818 XX X

Printed by C. Nicholls & Company Ltd
The Philips Park Press, Manchester
Design by Richard Hollis, GrR, and Roger Hart
Cover from photograph by John Sturrock, Report / London

Contents

To all my brothers and sisters

Preface and Acknowledgements

My work in the field of race relations has spanned ten years, but it would be optimistic to hope that these have been the worst ten years. I believe that racial conflict will become much worse in Britain. But academics are ill-placed to suggest solutions to social and political problems, so this book is a contribution to the activities of those who I hope will prove me to have been wrong.

Most of the first hand material is taken from the pages of *Race Today* or the reports of the Joint Council for the Welfare of Immigrants. Anne Dummett is mentioned; she wrote a book called *A Portrait of English Racism* (Penguin 1973) from which a few quotations are taken. With her husband Michael she also wrote a chapter in *Justice First* (Sheed and Ward 1969) which was probably one of the most important single pieces ever written about the politics of race relations. The discussion received no publicity because the publishers were too afraid of libel suits to publicise their book, which remained unreviewed and for which I never saw an advertisement. I have also drawn upon Stephen Castles and Godula Kosack, *Immigrant Workers and Class Structure in Western Europe* (OUP 1973), for my first chapter. The immigration figures are taken from Runnymede Trust publications and the official statistics.

Finally, I would like to thank Anne Alexander and Lindy Moore for their hard work and support in writing this book.

Aberdeen, November 1974

Introduction

David Oluwale was educated at a Roman Catholic school in Lagos; at the age of 19 he stowed away on a ship and came to England to study engineering. He received 28 days in Leeds jail for stowing away. Afterwards he found temporary work as a labourer and, in fact, never gained admission to college.

A friend remembered him as a 'popular young guy, a sharp dresser, excellent dancer'. Oluwale and his friends could not find regular work and fell foul of the police. They were constantly stopped in the streets and if they argued they were charged with obstruction.

In the early 1950s Oluwale got two months. From prison he was sent to a mental hospital where he remained for eight years. Four charges in 1965 gave him another two years in mental hospital and on release he received two sentences for 'wandering abroad'. The excellent dancer now shambled around the streets, the sharp dresser slept under paper in doorways. He became the object of further police attention. Harassment and brutality made his first and only aim in life one of avoiding the police. Two officers specialised in Oluwale-beating, other officers called them up on their radios when they spotted Oluwale. One of the specialists was said to go white and out of control whenever he saw Oluwale; they kicked him and beat him, they urinated on him.

In April 1969 David Oluwale's body was dragged from the river and two years later two policemen were charged with his manslaughter.

The judge warned the jury against accepting independent civilian witnesses' evidence against the police. The fact that the assailants wore police uniform did not prove that they were policemen. He asserted that the charge of perjury against one of the defendants had not been proven – even though another officer confessed to helping prepare a false duty book entry when Oluwale had been charged with assault. The police, the judge said, 'do their best to enable people like you and me to sleep in our beds in safety'. Oluwale was 'a menace to society, a nuisance to the police, a frightening apparition to come across at night'. The policemen were convicted on the lesser charges of assault.

The frightening apparition was a product of police harassment, prison and mental hospital. How could an ambitious young man be brought to this state and to a pauper's grave by policemen who found him a nuisance? He certainly did not like authority, but this was because landlords, policemen and labour exchange officials had a place for him in society that he would not accept, because he wanted to improve himself. So he had to be controlled and *taught* his place.

How do we explain the behaviour of the men who helped him to his grave at the age of 39? Were there just two bad apples in the police barrel? David Oluwale can be seen as typical of the black man in Britain: arriving full of hope, finding neither work nor a decent home, treated as trash, rebelling, trying to stand up for his manhood by resisting authority, and being pursued and crushed by that authority. That death in spring 1969 is not explained by naming the vindictive policeman and declaring him mad. It is explained by Ron Phillips when he wrote of the life and death of David Oluwale in *Race Today*: 'If the entire society defines a group as a threat, then the police forces have a vested interest in reducing that threat by a positive policy of attack'. So the officers responsible for the death of 'one lame darkie' represent *all* authority, they 'would have been acting on behalf of a society which has indicated time and time again that it would prefer blacks to disappear, either

2

into the ghettos of a suppressed sub-proletariat or in some other way'.

The pattern of exploitation suffered by blacks in this country is not accidental but part and parcel of the very nature of the society in which we live. To understand the conditions of blacks in particular – and migrant workers in general – we have to understand the part they are made to play in economic, social and political affairs. The first chapter explains why workers and families leave their home country and why they come to Britain and other European countries. The second chapter examines the way in which British Commonwealth black immigrants have come to be defined as a 'problem', the political campaigns mounted against them and the legislation that has stripped them of their rights and made them much more like rightless alien workers and foreign workers in the European Community. If Ron Phillips was right in his judgement of what happens once a group is defined as a problem then we might expect to find that official attitudes to coloured people include some positive elements of the hostility and 'attack' that he mentions. Chapter three shows how this has been the case in respect of the immigration authorities, who bring considerable and unnecessary hardship to intending immigrants and their families. Chapter four continues the discussion by describing the way in which the police and the courts behave towards coloured people. In these two chapters we will discover that Oluwale's death was not 'accidental'; it was the outcome of a pattern of relations well-established by officialdom and which is justified by the politicians' definition of the black as a problem.

Chapter five describes the actual experience of immigrants at work and thus puts flesh and blood upon the general discussion of the first chapter. Here we see something of the hostility of the white trade unions but also the variability of trade unions' attitudes in different industries and on different issues. One thing emerges from this chapter quite clearly, namely blacks are fighting back. The last part of the chapter

3

takes the discussion of the fight back from the place of work into the community and looks at some of the more and some of the less successful ways in which blacks try to overcome oppression and dehumanisation.

But many readers will have a vague feeling that all cannot be bad because successive governments have tried to do 'positive' things to help coloured people. The feelings are vague because people neither see nor feel the effects of these policies in their daily lives. So the discussion of this is put in an Appendix, for those who want to read about it. Some of the main facts are set out. It will be seen that even within the 'race relations industry' there is something of a black resistance developing.

A policeman thought it appropriate that David Oluwale 'went for a swim' and I have tried to show how a man can come to think in this way. But we should also ask ourselves if the forces at work in society that destroyed David Oluwale are very different from the forces that reduce many other people, white as well as black, to misery and hopelessness. Might not more of us go 'for a swim' in one way or another because of these forces? The answers to these questions are neither obvious nor simple and readers may come to contrary conclusions on the basis of this book. Whatever the conclusions readers come to it is important that they ask the questions. To discuss and debate the questions would be a step towards resolving them.

1.

'We're here because you were there'

Britain has received many generations of immigrants. Modern immigration began in the nineteenth century with the arrival of thousands of Irish men and women; more and more Irish people had to leave their country because of the great starvation following the failures of the 1847 and 1848 potato harvests. Irish workers dug canals and railways, they sank mine shafts and unloaded ships when the rise of modern industry created a demand for labour which could not be met from within Britain alone.

There has also been a more recent migration, which many people think of as being mainly of black people. Perhaps we have not tried to understand this migration: we have commonly treated it as some kind of natural disaster which we would have avoided if it could have been foreseen.

Trying to understand the facts about migration into Britain means looking beyond our own shores, to compare our experience with the overall pattern of migration into Europe and to grasp the relationship between the European countries which receive immigrants and the countries from which the immigrants came.

During recent years about 11 million migrant workers have moved into the industrial north-west of Europe. The largest numbers have migrated to France (over 3 million), West Germany (just under 3 million) and Great Britain (2.6 million). The proportion of migrant workers is high in Switzerland, Belgium and Luxembourg although the actual numbers are smaller in these countries. But the numbers and proportions

Black Commonwealth workers compared with all British workers

Immigrant percentage high compared with British in:	% of black Commonwealth labour force	% of British labour force
Metal work	1.81	0.85
Engineering	12.45	11.14
Textiles	3.14	1.63
Clothing	4.09	1.88
Other manufacturing	2.65	1.35
Labouring	11.43	5.19
Professional workers	13.58	9.55
More or less equal		
Service workers	11.12	12.04
Percentage low compared with British in:		
Construction	0.82	2.39
Clerical	9.81	13.69
Sales	3.42	9.59
Administration	1.47	3.08

are misleading when taken alone because migrants are mainly young men who are active in the labour force, whereas the native population includes children, women and old people, all of whom are much less active in the work force. Immigrants as a proportion of the total labour force are as follows.

Norway: 1.2 per cent
Denmark: 1.7 per cent
Belgium/Netherlands/Luxemburg: 4.6 per cent
Sweden: 5.6 per cent
Britain: 6.5 per cent
France: 8.3 per cent
W. Germany: 8.7 per cent
Switzerland: 30 per cent

The figure for Switzerland is quite remarkable. So much of Switzerland's manual work is done by foreign workers that Swiss children seldom think of taking a manual occupation when they leave school.

The migrant workers are not evenly spread through the work force, but concentrated in particular sectors of industry, notably the car industry. In West Germany 50 per cent of all motor-car assembly line workers are immigrants; in France, almost 40 per cent. The Volvo motor works in Sweden employs about 45 per cent immigrants, and Volvo's language teaching programme adds about £5 to the cost of every car. The West Midlands of England, an area based largely on car manufacture, is also an area of heavy immigrant population: nearly 15 per cent of the British black population lives in the West Midlands, compared with 5 per cent of the white population.

But migrants do not work only in manufacturing. While 11,000 out of the 17,000 workers in the BMW factory in Munich are Turks, virtually *all* the street sweepers are Turkish. In Switzerland, 40 per cent of all factory workers, but between 50 and 60 per cent of all hotel workers, are foreign. In Britain, black workers are found in the transport services and the hospitals, and many European migrants in the hotel and catering industries. Hospital orderlies for the German hospital service are recruited from the Philippines and South Korea. The service sector is renowned for its low wages and poor working conditions, and some European countries also use migrant labour on the land – another low-wage industry. Switzerland actually has regulations preventing migrant workers from leaving jobs in catering and agriculture, a sure indication of low pay and poor conditions.

Migrant workers are used largely to fill jobs that native workers will not do, because of their low wages or low esteem. And yet they are jobs which are essential to the maintenance of basic public services and which bolster up our consumer economy. Migrant workers operate much of Britain's public transport; they staff hospitals, clean schools, offices and public

7

buildings; they work in catering, construction and productive industry. In the West Riding, for example, the introduction of new and expensive machinery into the woollen industry necessitated new kinds of shift working which were unacceptable to the traditional labour force of local women. The unacceptable shifts are now largely operated by Pakistanis directly recruited from Pakistan by the employers. Thus the survival of the industry and the economic development of the region depended on migrant workers. This kind of story could be repeated throughout Europe. Willy Brandt, the former West German Chancellor, went so far as to say that Germany's 'economic miracle' was built on the labour of the 'guestworkers'. In fact, Germany's and Europe's great postwar prosperity has been built on a combination of labour and cheap raw materials from the less developed countries.

There are other reasons why migrant labour has been useful to Europe. As a German employer put it: 'The great value of the employment of foreigners lies in the fact that we thus have a mobile labour potential at our disposal.' The last three words are important; the migrant worker is not a free agent. He may fill slots in the labour market – taking unwanted jobs or making up the labour shortage – but he is essentially at the disposal of the employer or government of the country in which he is working. He has no right of residence, he is not a full citizen, he can be expelled from the country. Thus with the onset of the oil crisis in late 1973 Germany anticipated unemployment in the motor-car and chemical industries by ceasing to allow in Turkish workers, and the European press actively discussed the possibility and problems of expelling migrant workers.

Disposability can also work on a seasonal basis: in Switzerland you can only build for 9 months of the year, so the migrant workers are dismissed at the end of the season and have to return home. They are re-engaged at the beginning of the next season. But by breaking their residence they never qualify for Swiss social security benefits. So the Swiss gain from mig-

8

rant building labour without it ever becoming a charge on their state.

In general, despite variations from country to country, the migrant worker in Europe lacks formal rights of citizenship such as the right to vote and the right to residence, and, in many cases, the right to full social benefits. There may be a limit on the worker's stay, especially if he is on a fixed contract. There may be restrictions on his ability to change jobs or place of residence. Permission normally has to be sought to change job or residence. Unemployment may, and usually does, lead to the worker having to leave the country. The worker is peculiarly dependent on his employer, because of his fear of being sent home to a country lacking jobs and opportunities. The lack of a vote also makes the migrant politically weaker than his native counterpart, and he will find it extremely difficult to form a trade union, given the hostility of local unions and the ability of employers virtually to deport 'troublesome' workers.

A French magazine recently reported that immigrant workers, including civil rights activists and union leaders, had 'been put forcibly on to a boat and a plane to take them back to their country of origin' because 'they were pressing for improved living and working conditions'. A clergyman was also under an expulsion order because he had asked the French government if immigrant workers had to 'remain silent, with folded arms, in the face of the misery and injustice under which foreign workers suffer'. Large numbers of Portuguese workers in the catering trade in London have been subject to this kind of situation; to breathe the word 'union' has for a long time been to invite a one-way trip back to Portugal. The very fact that it is possible for employers to get rid of workers in this way gives the employer a very much greater degree of control over the migrant than he would have over a local worker.

In addition to these handicaps the worker is unlikely to receive more than elementary training and certainly only slight promotion from his employer. To train or promote a worker is to make him less disposable. So when we hear of discrimination in employment we should not automatically think that something has gone wrong; it follows from the way in which migrant labour is used in the Western European economy that it should be discriminated against in training and promotion.

As if political and economic handicaps were not enough, the European migrant worker suffers a further deprivation. The European governments place very strict limitations on the entry of families. Thus the migrant worker lives apart from his family. This too is useful; the worker is more mobile and disposable, more likely to work uncongenial hours than he would if settled with his wife and children. To allow the migrant to settle with his family, to train and promote him, is to throw away the economic advantages of the use of migrant workers. The terms and conditions of the migrant's entry are geared *entirely* to the needs of the receiving society and not to the needs of the migrant.

Bad housing is another striking result of the migrant's lack of economic, political and domestic security. Municipal housing is not so well developed in continental Europe as in Britain and Scandinavia; the migrant worker is therefore not likely to qualify for public housing. Meanwhile he is unlikely to have the funds to rent a flat on the private market, let alone buy or take a mortgage on a private house. Various 'solutions' to this problem are adopted. In Switzerland and Germany there is a growing market in illegal lettings of attics and basements to migrant workers. Complaints about conditions in such lettings have led to the deportation of the people complaining. In Germany also some employers provide hostels. Hostels are common in France, and there are many which do not conform to building or health regulations. Hostels run by employers have an added disadvantage in that they enable the employer to extend his supervision and control of the worker from the workplace into the home. This situation is acute when the hostel is actually within the factory premises – the hostel is then similar to a colonial labour compound, as still found in South Africa. Some French hostels for Algerian workers have wardens who are white settlers returned from Algeria. This, plus poor conditons, has led to complaints and organised protest which have resulted in the riot police attacking the hostels and the leading complainants being deported. It is not surprising that about a third of all Algerians in France live in cafés and hotels.

Shanty towns (*bidonvilles*), often built on or near re-development sites with the materials to hand, house over 75,000 people in France. The erection of *bidonvilles* is the worst possible 'solution' to the problem of the lack of housing. The shacks lack any domestic facilities and the shanty town lacks normal urban amenities. From time to time the shanty towns are bulldozed, only to arise elsewhere. Needless to say the existence of the shanty towns and the response of the French authorities to them give rise to considerable conflict.

In Britain one source of conflict, certainly in the mid-1960s, was the practice of multi-occupation by immigrant workers. This was one way in which men coped with the housing shortage by buying up large houses unwanted on the local market. Men could then share the accommodation and cooking facilities and let parts of it in order to pay off the debt incurred in the purchase. The rapid and inevitable deterioration of property used in this way was associated in many people's minds with urban decay, for which migrants were blamed. Other migrant workers, especially those with families, bought small terraced houses and some, in spite of discrimination, gained local authority housing. There are quite marked regional and local variations in immigrant housing patterns in Britain, especially after the imposition of immigration restrictions which encouraged migrants to bring their families in to settle. Throughout Europe, however, migrant workers have tended to congregate in particular parts of towns and cities, initially because accommodation is to be found there. Later arrivals join friends or fellow-countrymen. Soon shops, cinemas, places of worship and cafés grow up to cater for national needs and thus 'little Italies' or 'coloured quarters' grow to be a feature of most European cities. This also means that the migrant communities are isolated and identifiable.

In summary, the migrant worker in Europe is relatively rightless compared with local citizens, he is dependent on employers and government, he is disposable and closely supervised, sometimes in his private life as well as at work. He does jobs for which there is no labour available or which locals will not do. He is probably without his family and forced to house himself on the margins of the private housing market, illicitly, or in a hostel.

This may not seem to describe the typical migrant in Britain – but it does in fact describe the situation of about a third of the migrant force in Britain: the alien non-Commonwealth workers. The next chapter will describe how new migrants from the Commonwealth will in the future be in a position much more like that of the alien worker.

What I have described so far is the development of two labour markets in the European economy. In the first market, men and women are, formally and legally, free to sell their labour for the best price they can get to whoever they please. This freedom is modified by the compulsion of hunger and the practical difficulties of constantly changing jobs and residence, but it is a freedom nevertheless. The freedom is defended and enlarged to some extent by the development of trade unions which enable wage bargaining to be carried out collectively – thus increasing the market power of large numbers of unionised workers. Workers also have formal political movements and parliamentary parties which seek through organised methods to change the rules by which market bargaining takes place; recent struggles over the Industrial Relations Act are an example of conflict over the rules by which labour will maintain its bargaining position.

In contrast to this system, there are several forms of unfree labour. In the extreme case there is slavery, but also indentured labour, on the plantations of the colony. Also, and especially in the colony, there is the labour compound in which migrant rural workers forced off the best land by the settlers, and off the poor land left for them through poverty and high taxes, are forced to live as bachelors for many months of the year and many years of their lives. They work in the mine and send money home, occasionally seeing their families. Unions are not allowed and even recreation is supervised by the company. These are forms of labour in which a very high degree of compulsion and occasionally physical force are used to keep men at work. Men may not sell their labour freely: they are their employer's personal property permanently or for a limited period; or the kinds of jobs they may do and the wages they receive are limited and fixed by law. They are tied to an employer and may be brought back forcibly, or denied any further employment if they try to change jobs.

But now this *unfree* labour has become part of the European labour scene. In this chapter I have described men who are not free to sell their labour as they choose in the free market and who lack the political rights of citizens as a basis upon which to organise themselves to gain a more secure foothold in the labour market. They are employed at the employer's will alone, and he holds all the trump cards when dealing with migrant workers.

The implications of this are clear. The presence of the new unfree worker changes the structure of European society. We have a traditional working class with rights embodied in trade unions, legal codes, social security provisions and defended by political parties. But below them are the rightless workers with no such laws and institutions to protect them. This sub-proletariat of rightless workers can be used to insulate the local working class from fluctuations in the economy by being 'last in and first out' in boom and recession, while keeping essential public services going all the time. But migrant workers could be used to replace local workers who through traditional trade union methods have achieved wages that employers are unwilling to pay. In fact some employers prefer to export the work to cheap-labour areas rather than to import the labour. Two American employers have recently moved 5,000 jobs from America to Taiwan (Formosa) and thus closed down home opportunities, and some UK companies have closed works in Britain while opening others in South Africa.

The European working class has always benefited from the relatively forced labour of the colonies and the supply of cheap raw materials from European overseas territories. Today it is benefiting from the exploitation of ex-colonial workers *at home* in a situation of economic crisis and rising domestic conflict. Race conflict thus becomes a new facet of domestic unrest; no European country has avoided it, although so far such conflict has not erupted with quite the same vigour in Scandinavia as in the rest of Europe. *Divide and rule* on a racial basis could become a domestic tactic of European employers and governments. This is certainly a background factor of some importance to bear in mind when reading the next chapter.

But why do migrants come to Europe at all ? They come for jobs, high wages and to seek a future for themselves and their children. They come from poor countries: the Mediterranean countries and the ex-colonial nations, including Ireland. In the case of the ex-colonies a country is often poor because the colonisers 'developed' it to meet the needs of the home country; in some cases this meant a demand for a single crop (sugar, rubber or cocoa) or a single mineral (gold or copper). Even when Britain gives aid to underdeveloped countries it is to enable them to buy our goods, seldom to help them industrialise themselves. Aid builds roads and hydro-electric schemes, or even factories, but these enable us to use their resources cheaply or their labour more effectively for our own purposes. Again, a number of ex-colonies, like the Mediterranean countries, are being opened up for tourism. This means vast profits for European property companies and airlines, while for the locals it provides work as cooks, waiters or maids – or other non-productive activity like taxi-driving and prostitution.

Economic inequalities and simple poverty are now perpetuated by the way in which ex-colonies are related to the European Community. For example the ex-colonial powers will receive cheap raw materials from their ex-colonies, while the ex-colonies will have to admit manufactured goods from the EEC, thus doubly retarding their industrial growth. Some of the abler men in the colonies had no place in their own country because they were denied access to positions of influence or authority by the colonial power. They therefore sought their futures in Europe. The current exploitation of labour is just another aspect of the general exploitation of the poor countries by the rich countries. For example Britain has made an exception of doctors in its limitation on coloured immigration from 1965 onwards, thus enabling the National Health Service to recruit doctors from parts of the world in far greater need of medical skills than Britain.

It is doubtful whether the income from migrants' remittances will ever replace the human potential lost by migration. Twenty per cent of Yugoslavia's total work force has left home. Dozens of villages in Pakistan, Turkey and Portugal are inhabited only by children, women and old men. Admittedly, the remittances can be considerable. A recent report in *Time* magazine said: 'In Spain, migrants' remittances are the second source of foreign-exchange income after tourism. In Yugoslavia, earnings sent home have turned a balance of payments deficit into a surplus and emigration has transformed a critical unemployment problem into one that is merely serious.' But this is hardly a recipe for economic success. For the larger and more distant ex-colonies like India and Pakistan the economic benefits of migration are negligible, especially when compared with the loss of skilled manpower, which ran at such a high level from Pakistan that the government had to restrict the emigration of school teachers.

What underlies the whole phenomenon of European migration is the gap between the rich and the poor countries. There are enormous worldwide financial interests that make considerable profit from the economic and political domination of the 'Third World'. We cannot expect eager support for the ending of relationships that maintain inequality and profit. But the fuel crisis has shown how much we depend on the reckless squandering of the resources of underdeveloped nations to maintain our way of life; and the sugar shortage of 1974 has revealed that we have been paying Commonwealth producers £83 a ton for sugar, when the world market price was nearly £400 a ton. Supposing all the producers of the goods we need got together like the oil-producing states and demanded a fair price for their goods? What then?

Migrants are here because our rulers created the conditions in their homelands which made migration necessary, as well as a situation in Europe into which migration was possible. In addition, the employers of Europe actively recruit throughout the poor nations. In both long and short term the answer can be given in the words of a friend from Sri Lanka who said: 'We are over here because you were over there.'

2.
Politicians
and the numbers game

There are some very arresting features in the British situation which remain baffling even after the general European situation is understood. Why is it, for example, that London Transport has to take buses and underground trains out of service while the very people deprived of these services clamour for a ban on the immigration of potential bus and train crews? Why is it that British hospitals advertise for nurses in the Oslo daily newspapers when there are many English-speaking women in the West Indies eager to train as nurses? Why does an exponent of the virtue of market forces like Enoch Powell advocate control of immigration, which is entirely subject to a market?

The answer to these questions lies in the peculiarly *racial* nature of the British 'debate' about immigration; in fact, it is something other than 'debate', because a debate assumes that two sides are heard.

Traditionally Britain has received labour from three sources, Ireland, Europe and the Commonwealth, in roughly equal proportions. The Irish have, in practice, been treated as if Ireland was a part of Britain. There has been free movement of labour on both a temporary and permanent basis. Even Irish people convicted of crimes and deported can, in effect, freely return to Britain. European workers have been treated in accordance with their status as aliens – they have been admitted conditionally to take jobs for which there is no British applicant, they stay on condition of good behaviour, have to be registered with the police and may apply for permanent residence. In fact as the number of Commonwealth migrants had declined, the number of short-stay aliens and 'aliens accepted for permanent residence' has increased.

Until 1962 Commonwealth immigrants could enter Britain freely to work or to settle; they enjoyed full rights as British citizens. In the Common Market, European workers lose some of their alien status; they may look for work in other EEC countries and settle if they they find it within three months. They must be employed under the same conditions as local workers and have full trade union and social security rights; wives and children under 21 may all join the migrant and settle. Commonwealth citizens who have not registered as UK citizens will not have the same mobility rights as other workers in the EEC.

British labour demand was met for a few postwar years by Polish workers, known as 'European voluntary workers', and workers from south and west Europe. From the early 1950s, however, Commonwealth workers began to feature in the migrant labour force in significant numbers. For the six years 1958 to 1963 Britain became a country with a net inward migration, when more people migrated into Britain than emigrated from Britain. During the early part of this short period a campaign was begun against black immigration – not *immigration* as such but *black* immigration.

The 1960s saw what has often been described as a 'Dutch auction' on race, in which each party tried to show that it was 'tougher' on coloured immigration than the other, each continually outbidding its opponent by adopting the other's policies. The rapidity of this 'auction' can be seen from the fact that in 1961 the Labour Party opposed Commonwealth immigration restriction as a matter of highest principle, yet in February 1965 a Labour Home Secretary could say: 'We have always been in favour of control.' In the 1970 election campaign, James Callaghan responded to a Powell speech by boasting how low he had squeezed the figures for black immigration, rather than attacking Powell for his hostility to black people. In 1965 Harold Wilson, a Labour Prime Minister, introduced a White Paper on Commonwealth immigration which contained all the principles on which a full colour bar was subsequently to be erected.

How did this all happen? It is worth retracing the steps which led to the present situation, because it is an object lesson in the way in which social policy can develop. Moreover, the way in which immigration policy was introduced helps explain the notoriously vicious and repressive way in which it has been put into effect. The history is especially interesting because the anti-black forces have been completely victorious. Most British political developments contain considerable elements of compromise; but this is not the case in immigration legislation. The moderate, liberal and non-racist forces were quite ineffective and achieved no compromise whatsoever. There can rarely have been such a complete victory (or defeat) for any political principle in Britain before or since.

Part of the problem lay in the veneer of liberalism that was common until the early 1960s. Because British immigration policy towards the Commonwealth asserted the idea of the brotherhood of man it was thought unnecessary to make any provision for black immigrants arriving in Britain. This lack of planning meant that the operation of the free labour market drew migrants to specific areas. In these areas unchecked racial discrimination led to the development of areas of 'black' housing, which in turn created a concentration of black children in the schools when wives and children joined black immigrants.

It was also true, of course, that in areas like London and the West Midlands the presence of *black* and therefore *visible* immigrants showed up problems that had already existed and for which the migrants themselves were not to blame: shortage of housing, inadequate health and education services and so on. (No-one would seriously suggest that Britain had solved its housing problem by the time black immigration got under way.) It was easy in this situation to blame the black population for the problems with which they were apparently associated. The result of the policy of doing nothing and letting things drift along was that pressure began to mount from some local authorities to restrict black immigration. This also found local grass-roots support, and local resentments were further fed through active anti-coloured campaigning by the fascist fringe.

●

The 1962 Commonwealth Immigration Act

The main provision was to limit the entry of Commonwealth workers to those holding one of three types of employment voucher:

Category A:
People with specific jobs to come to in the UK. These vouchers were issued to the employers, but the others were issued to intending immigrants by the British High Commission in their own country.

Category B:
Persons with recognised skills or qualifications which are in short supply in the UK.

Category C:
All other persons; priority to those who served in the war and then on the basis of 'first come, first served'. The wife and children under 16 of voucher holders were also permitted to enter the UK.

Not all vouchers issued were taken up and used, but about 7,000 A vouchers were issued up to the end of 1963, and 5,100 B vouchers. A very large number of applications for Category C vouchers were received, so in mid-1963 and again in July 1974 there were cutbacks in the distribution of such vouchers. Category C was abolished in the 1965 White Paper, *Immigration from the Commonwealth*.

●

Figure 1: Workers and dependants admitted in a year
(thousands)

	1965	1966	1967	1968	1969	1970	1971
White Commonwealth	4	4	4	3	3	4	4
Black Commonwealth*	53	46	58	56	34	26	23
Foreign	102	110	102	98	100	102	94
Total	159	160	164	157	137	132	121

Figure 2: Migration into the United Kingdom 1963–1971
(thousands)

Source of Migration	1963	1964	1965	1966	1967	1968	1969	1970	1971
White Commonwealth									
Voucher holders	1	1	1					1	1
Dependants	2	2	2	3	3	2	3	2	2
Others	1	1	1	1	1	1		1	1
Total	4	4	4	(4)	(4)	(3)	(3)	4	4
Black Commonwealth*									
Voucher holders	29	14	12	5	5	4	4	3	2
Dependants	24	36	39	39	50	42	28	21	19
Others	3	3	2	2	3	4	2	2	2
Total	56	53	53	46	58	50	34	26	23
Foreign									
Permit holders	6	9	10	9	7	9	10	8	9
Dependants	2	3	3	3	2	2	3	3	4
Others	7	7	7	7	8	9	9	9	11
Total	15	19	20	19	17	20	22	20	24
Foreigners admitted for less than a year			21	23	23	22	25	23	19
Totals	(75)	(76)	98	(92)	(102)	(97)	(84)	73	70

*Excluding UK Passport holders from East Africa

Immigration statistics are notoriously difficult to interpret (and easy to misrepresent). Figures 1 and 2 show how small a proportion of all migration is made up of black settlers and suggest also that a high proportion of these are the dependants of Voucher holders admitted before 1966.

The first action to deal with the situation was the passing of the 1962 Commonwealth Immigration Act. This introduced a system of vouchers related to different kinds of job opportunity. The numbers of vouchers issued was controlled. The lowest grade, 'C', was gradually reduced until abolished by the Wilson White Paper in 1965. An immediate consequence of the

All migration – temporary and to settle

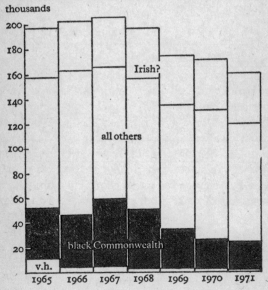

v.h. = black Commonwealth voucher holders

22

Migration for settlement 1963-71
(excluding Irish)

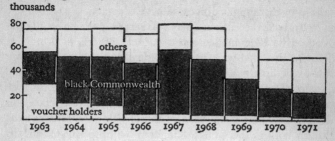

thousands

introduction of the Bill, which became the 1962 Act, was an upsurge of Commonwealth immigration as potential immigrants decided to 'beat the ban'. This fuelled the fires of those who said that there was an immigration problem. If *all* immigration had been restricted and tough anti-discrimination measures had been introduced, the subsequent history of race relations in Britain might have been different. But even at this early stage some Labour MPs must have felt grass-roots pressure on them to restrict black migration, because there was a very low turnout of Labour MPs to vote against the 1962 Act.

Two points have to be made on this stage of the story; firstly, from here on, whatever the words used, the campaign was against *black* immigration. There has never been any public discussion of immigration or immigration control; the facts have never been put before the public. Thus today an 'immigrant' is usually taken to mean a black man and 'immigration control' usually means a colour bar. Secondly, the 1962 Act encouraged migration and settlement. Whereas before some men in West Pakistan had migrated on a rotating basis within a family, they now decided to settle and bring their families to Britain. Others who may have hoped 'one day' to migrate migrated to 'beat the ban'. There was a similar immigration rush before the 1968 Act. Both these rushes then resulted in a long and large 'tail' of dependants in subsequent years.

23

In other words the Acts partially worsened the situation they were supposed to remedy and led to a more disorganised migration than might otherwise have occurred.

In 1964 the Labour Party was returned to power, but the prospective Foreign Secretary, Patrick Gordon Walker, was defeated in Smethwick by a candidate who adopted a strong anti-black immigration line. From late 1964 until mid-1965 the Conservative Party began to discuss very much tougher measures against black immigration, including restrictions on Commonwealth immigration to those with parents or grandparents born in the United Kingdom – a proposal that was to reappear later.

●

Harold Wilson's White Paper, 'Immigration from the Commonwealth' 1965

The annual issue of Category A and B vouchers to be cut to 8,500 with 1,000 reserved for Malta.

Stricter tests of eligibility for the entry of children aged 16–18.

Home Secretary given powers to deport at his discretion, without a court ruling, any immigrant of less than five year's standing, who he considered had flouted the immigration regulations.

●

In August 1965 Wilson introduced his White Paper and in one move upstaged both the Conservative Party and his own specialist committee which was looking into immigration and race. The 1965 White Paper came at the end of a period of increasingly strident debate about black immigration. There were public incidents involving petitions against black residents in particular areas or burning crosses being fixed to black citizens' doors, and there was a rising tide of hysterical anti-black letters in the national and local press.

There was thus a crisis in race relations arising from a combination of uncertainty over the meaning and implications of black immigration, government inaction, and a conscious anti-coloured campaign organised from the extremist fringe of the Conservative Party. A public policy statement by the new government was clearly going to be of the greatest significance. This was indeed the case. The Wilson White Paper was a disaster for race relations, because while it temporarily took the wind out of the sails of the anti-black campaigners, it did in fact implicitly concede all the major points in their case and it laid down principles on which all future legislation has been based and around which anti-black sentiments could be mobilised.

1. The White Paper conceded that black immigration *as such* was the problem.

2. It suggested that *numbers* were the essence of the solution to the problem and even went so far as to make the absurd suggestion that restricting black immigration would be good for race relations.

The basis of argument had clearly shifted. It was no longer possible to make statements about 'a small and over-crowded island' because the debate was plainly about black immigration only. No attempt was made to limit total immigration. Wilson therefore suggested that the problem of the black immigrant was that he was more of a burden on our social services than white citizens. This was quite untrue and research subsequently showed that the social services gained from an influx of young working taxpayers. But the argument served its purpose by providing a cloak of respectability to an otherwise openly anti-black measure.

The specific proposals were to restrict Commonwealth migration to 8,500 workers (plus dependants) every year, including 1,000 from Malta. The black person was thus identified as the source of 'the problem' that had to be dealt with. In effect, 'the fewer the better' was now the watchword. This was a major setback for the social workers, local councillors, politicians and others who in the face of rising hysteria had emphasised that social problems existed before migrants came from the black Commonwealth. These people had been insisting that social problems be tackled as social problems and that the public should not be diverted and divided into blaming black immigrants and into believing that the problems would be relieved by stopping coloured immigration. They were also afraid of the human consequences of raising hostility between black and white communities. The White Paper cut the ground from under their feet by appearing to give government backing to the view that it really was the black immigrants who were to blame. One social worker in the East End of London said that the White Paper destroyed 25 years of his life's work.

Publication of the White Paper marked the point at which the racist attitude began to harden, at which anti-black ideas became respectable and at which the final route of the liberals began. Anti-black politics moved into the reputable centre of the main parties. The White Paper bought a little time for the Labour government, but probably only because the anti-black elements were surprised by gaining so much. But even at the time the paper was published the question of a total ban on dependants was being discussed. The effect of anti-black legislation has always been to quieten the demands of the racists for a time only, while they reformulate their policies to cope with the new situation. It is impossible to buy off the extremists who will always want more, and impossible to re-assure the public when the extremists are out to alarm them on the basis of arguments which you have already conceded. In fact from the time of the White Paper onwards a rational debate about immigration and race was unwinnable. The White Paper had conceded so much ground to the extremists that no ground was left on which to resist them. Like the 1962 Act, the 1965 White Paper encouraged the extremists because they could now see that substantial gains were to be made. From here on even the meaning of words changed; in newspaper editorials and political speeches, what had been extremism was now 'commonsense', while calm and informed discussion became extremism or 'woolly idealism'.

The White Paper also gave the anti-black campaigners the ideal ground upon which to campaign. The question of *numbers* became central to the black immigration debate.

Once the debate is about numbers there are no issues of principle to be discussed, only *how many* ? In being drawn into this discussion, liberals allowed themselves to be drawn onto racist ground because they were unable to argue about principles but had to accept the contention that coloured people were basically the problem. You can no longer argue that there is nothing wrong with black immigration or that it is positively a good thing. Similarly arguments about how much we benefited from black immigrants were very dangerous because they implied that people were entitled to certain rights only because they were useful.

The argument about numbers is unwinnable because however many you decide upon there will always be someone to campaign for less and others for whom one is too many. Since you have admitted that black people are a problem in themselves, it is impossible to resist the argument for less of them. Even if new migrants are reduced to nil, the argument can be shifted to the numbers of dependants; when they are reduced it can be shifted to the question of illegal immigrants; when these are shown to be few in number it can be argued that the government is cooking the books. In the last analysis if you play the numbers game then black people already here and every black child born here is a problem and the discussion shifts to questions of deportation. What *might* happen has happened *in fact*, as anyone will know who reads his daily paper or who follows the race speeches of Enoch Powell. Today it is still a question of *how many* ? but this time the numbers will go up with rising repatriation demands.

It may seem as if people have gone mad when discussion

of public policy takes this kind of turn. It is quite puzzling that an exponent of the free operation of the market like Enoch Powell should play the restrictionist numbers game so assiduously. It also makes one wonder if politicians are unable to see the consequences of their actions.

Part of the answer is that politicians think in the short term; their main concern is to survive in power or to gain power. They will take almost any action to meet what they see as a threat to their survival and treat the consequences of that action as another problem later on if necessary. Wilson misjudged Smethwick: Gordon Walker was defeated because he was strongly disliked by the electorate, but that electorate was not truly represented by the vociferous anti-black minority. It was more fluid and uncertain. But Wilson acted in order to ensure his own survival as he saw it; in 1964 Labour had a tiny Commons majority. And when Wilson confirmed that black people were a problem and that too many were coming into the country, he transformed existing muted fears into alarm.

Secondly, there is the part played by specific anti-black sentiment. There has always been an extremist fringe to European politics; it contains some people who are filled with race hatred to the point of mental illness. Others have theories of racial superiority or experience resentment at the loss of empire and 'national greatness' and blame it on communists, people with long hair, students, blacks and others. There are also some people who in a reasoned and calculated way believe in a strong state, the suppression of subversive minorities, censorship and so on. They believe that 'lawless' elements like trade unions should be brought under control and that everybody should work, under compulsion if necessary, for a national good. They usually reserve to themselves the right to define what is good for the nation.

Such groupings (and they are uneasy groupings at times) find expression in extreme right-wing or fascist movements. They remain on the political fringe. They can come to the centre, however, in times of economic crisis when a government appears to lose control.

One feature of fascism is that it thrives in situations of open civil strife: it offers simple solutions and can readily mobilise for street fighting. Membership forms for fascist groups in Britain today make specific enquiries about military service and rank. When there is fighting in the streets, the advocates of the strong state have an opportunity to introduce powerfully repressive measures against political organisation and expression. Racial conflict might provide an ideal opportunity for some kind of politicians; they might deliberately ferment racial strife. There is a sense in which the tough 'law and order' men *need* disorder so that their views can be put into effect. The extreme right is well known for its attempts to provoke its opponents to violence in order to justify strong measures against them.

In Britain the fascist fringe has achieved limited successes. But in the field of race it has been remarkably successful. Ann Dummett, a writer on race relations, recently remarked: 'What Mosley proclaimed as National Front policy in 1950 has. become by 1971 a policy that many people who think of themselves as moderate, unprejudiced and honourable would hold with equanimity. "We must treat these people fairly, but we must send them home".'

The racist position on race has achieved respectability in about ten years. It has done this because it has found spokesmen *within* the existing political parties. Whether they were making serious racist policy proposals or just finding an excuse to give vent to anti-black feelings, these politicians have brought racist policies in from the fringe to the centre of politics. Given also that each party was looking for ways to outdo the other, the fringe has been able to feed its policies to politicians eager for new vote-winning ideas. In particular, the Monday Club has played a very significant role in providing a bridge between the fascist fringe and the centre of the Tory Party. That this link has now become obvious seems to be leading to its breakdown, but not before a lot of anti-black traffic has passed over the bridge.

The 'numbers game' provides an easy link between an apparently reasoned and fair approach to immigration and the more radically anti-black position. So we indeed find 'fair-minded people' saying today what Mosley said fifteen years ago.

Anti-black agitation continued after the 1956 White Paper; by the end of 1967 it had focused on the Asians in Africa who had British citizenship. These were people who were offered the choice of British citizenship when the East African states achieved independence. It had been known and intended for many years that they had the right to enter the United Kingdom and settle. The agitation that grew around this led to an upsurge of migration, especially from Kenya at the turn of 1967/68. This produced the 1968 Commonwealth Immigration Act; again, the story shows how racial agitation can generate its own justification. The Act dropped all pretence of being non-racial. It deprived holders of British passports of the fundamental right of a citizen to reside in the country of his citizenship, unless they had a grandfather or parent born in the UK. As most whites in the Commonwealth have at least a grandfather born in the UK and most black citizens do not, it was plain what the Act was meant to do. The 'grandfather clause' is a well-known device, first used in the middle of the last century in America to prevent blacks getting the vote.

For once a vigorous opposition was mounted to the Act, even though the Labour government rushed it through parliament in record time. The Bill passed through both Houses of Parliament and received the Royal Assent in two days; and airlines were applying the Act before it even became law.

There was some confusion during its passage through Parliament, due, to some extent, to opponents of the Bill being better informed than the government, who were legislating in great haste. For example government spokesmen were quite unable to agree on the numbers of potential immigrants in-volved. In the Commons Callaghan said that 200,000 might come from East Africa but the Lord Chancellor thought the figure was 243,000 (HofL Col 925). Under pressure Lord Gardiner upped the total to 2.43 million but later reduced it to 1.2 million. Lord Kilbracken observed that anyone could play this absurd game if one counted simple numbers without considering who might want to come to Britain. Why not add the Irish to the Lord Chancellor's million and make the figure 4 million? (HofL 1078). The most widely accepted total for East African Asians was 156,000.

The figures were not entirely intended to inform: the Lord Chancellor, in common with other supporters of the Act, raised the spectre of a million Chinese who might invade from Malaysia if the Bill was not passed. This was the entire population of the ex-colonies of Penang and Malacca with *dual* nationality, unlike the East African Asians who held UK passports only (HofL 925, 1077). Duncan Sandys looked forward to 'a massive exodus of Chinese refugees' from Hong Kong and saw the Act as necessary to stop them. Were these figures presented to inform or to alarm and thereby hasten the Bill through? Others, like Lord Brooke, relied upon equally crude threats of 'the explosion that would follow in towns and cities where the number of immigrants have already reached near-saturation point' (Col 944) or Lord Wigg who feared 'scenes of disorder of the kind that disfigured Dudley' (Col 965). The noble Lords were, of course, only expressing the 'ordinary working-class point of view' (Col 1021). In fact one of the most discreditable aspects of this debate was the claim that it was the public rather than the government that was prejudiced.

Many other 'facts' were wrong. The Solicitor General, for example, asserted that the 'ancestral connection' of most UK passport holders would be 'through the paternal line' (HofC Col 1426) but he was quite unable to substantiate this when the sexual discrimination built into the Bill was challenged. Some speakers quoted dubious sources (Cols 1019–20), others just told lies (HofC 1278, HofL 1076).

Accused of racism the government, in the person of Lord

Stonham, pointed out that the Bill applied to the Welsh settled in Patagonia and the Scots in the Argentine (HofL 1120). But under pressure his answers revealed the government's basic 'kith and kin' motivation. To bring all Commonwealth citizens under the provision of the Act would, he said, 'offend many people with close family connections with this country' (Col 1212). The fact that most of these were white was a matter of geography, not race.

In the House of Lords the government made no attempt to answer the critics. Instead the government maintained a very general debate at a very emotional level, with constant references to the 'yellow peril' kind of argument. The opponents of the Bill won the day with their arguments in both Houses, but the government won the votes. Racism not reason carried the day.

Confusion, evasions, lies and contradictions of a kind that have come to typify the discussion of race in Britain marked this debate. Race is not an area in which ministers of either party now feel any obligation to tell the truth – especially as those who suffer from their actions are largely out of sight and out of mind.

The 1968 Act, passed at the beginning of Human Rights Year, created thousands of stateless persons overnight; it has led to the imposition of hardship and suffering on a scale almost unequalled by British legislation in recent years. Much of it will never be known; little of it ever qualifies as 'news'. It will be discussed in the next chapter, which describes how the immigration laws have been applied.

The 1968 Act is currently under the scrutiny of the European Human Rights Commission at Strasbourg, as its provisions appear to be in breach of the European Convention on Human Rights, to which the British government put its name. As British citizens the East African Asians have been able to appeal to Strasbourg; other Commonwealth citizens have not had this opportunity, although their human rights have been abused in the same way.

The final landmark in the development of the immigration colour bar was the 1971 Immigration Act. This changed the status of most Commonwealth immigrants to that of aliens. The Act divides people into 'patrials' and 'non-patrials', which almost means whites and non-whites. Patrials are British passport holders who were born in this country or whose parents were born here; they have the 'right of abode' in Britain. This means that the Act opens the door to immigration wider than at any time since restriction began, because it grants unlimited rights of entry to millions of Commonwealth whites. For example, 2.4 million whites have emigrated to the Commonwealth since 1945 alone; they, their children and grandchildren now have the right to settle in Britain. Thus Robert Carr was not telling the truth when he said that the Conservative government had restricted immigration more fully than any previous government. Not quite all patrials will be white because British passport holders who were adopted, naturalised or registered here or who have lived here for five years and are accepted for permanent residence also qualify as patrial – and these categories will include some black citizens.

●

The 1968 Immigration Act

Removed right of entry of British passport holders unless they had a 'substantial connection' with the UK – ie, at least one grandparent born here. Act may have been in contravention of European Human Rights Convention.

●

The 1971 Commonwealth Immigration Act

1. *Removes* all controls on immigration of Commonwealth citizens who have at least one British-born grandparent.

2. No others have right to enter the UK; they need permission to enter and need a work permit for a specific job with a specific employer. Admitted for one year and permission may be renewed for three more years at Home Secretary's discretion.

3. Dependants have no right of entry but may be admitted for duration of work permit only.

4. Commonwealth immigrants subject to control have to register with the Department of Employment.

5. The power of deportation extended and deportable 'offences' made retrospective. One-time illegal immigrants, no longer subject to deportation, may now be deported.

●

A non-patrial Commonwealth citizen has no right to settle or bring dependants. He will need a work permit for a specific job in a specific place for a specific period (usually twelve months). At the end of a year he may apply for an extension to stay and after four years he may apply to register as a British citizen free of conditions. For this application to be granted the applicant must, among other things, be of 'good character' (as defined by the Home Office). Like the alien, the non-patrial will need permission to change jobs, but he has to register with the Department of Employment rather than the police and he retains his vote.

It will be seen from this that the non-patrial (mainly black) migrant will now be very much at the mercy of the employer, police and Home Office. The Home Secretary also has powers to deport those whose presence is 'not conducive to the public good'. It is widely believed that these powers will be used to deter civil rights and trade union activism amongst future immigrant workers.

This Act was also passed very hurriedly, in fulfilment of election promises. Responsible ministers do not seem to be able to interpret the Act fully and at times they contradict themselves and one another. A further complication is that some of the Act's provisions are contrary to the Treaty of Rome and will probably be revised, although there is evidence to suggest that there is an agreement between European governments not to interfere in one another's anti-immigrant legislation. The Act, for example, gives the Home Secretary greater delegated power over immigration than he is allowed by the Treaty of Rome. This is but one example of confusion and contradiction in the field of immigration control.

The Labour government which came to power in March 1974 might have been expected to repeal the 1971 Act. The new Home Secretary, Roy Jenkins, had said of the Act, when in opposition:

> 'This is a highly objectionable Bill. It is misconceived in principle and damaging in practice. It is liable to make not merely every new coloured immigrant or every existing immigrant, but also every coloured person born in this country, feel less secure, less wanted and less belonging, thus inevitably exacerbating community relations. If the Government had any self-respect, they would withdraw the Bill and start again.'

But once in government, Jenkins seemed unable to grasp the wisdom of his own words and settled instead for making the operation of the Act marginally more humane. The new immigration rules issued after the 1971 Act also export our racism to other European countries, because if Dutch or French citizens gained their citizenship by birth in Dutch or French ex-colonies, Britain does not recognise or treat them as citizens for the purposes of immigration control.

Given the need for labour it is not altogether surprising that employers turn to alternative sources. So today we find the following headlines in our papers: 'Imported factory girls live nine in a room', 'House-girls – live on £6 a week', 'Scandal of imported women workers', 'UK clothing trade running migrants' sweat shop.' South and West Europe is becoming an increasing source of labour, but the Philippines also provided domestic servants, hospital orderlies and textile workers. We can see why the buses and London Underground still lack workers – they need English-speaking staff who cannot be provided by Portugal or the Philippines.

It is impossible to obtain forecasts of migrant labour demand from relevant government departments; they claim to have no policy on the matter. This is hardly surprising, since governments which have gone to so much trouble to keep non-whites out are unlikely to admit that there is nevertheless a great need for migrant labour.

It might be thought that so much apparent malice could not possibly come from supposedly responsible governments. Two examples will show malice towards black citizens in its purest form. Both took place under the 1966 Labour government.

In 1969 an Immigration Appeals Act was introduced to set up appeal procedures for intending immigrants who were refused entry to the United Kingdom. On 16 May, late in the third reading, the Home Secretary, James Callaghan, introduced a measure which made it obligatory for intending immigrants to obtain an entry certificate from the British authorities in *their home country*. No appeals machinery was to be provided overseas. Thus a very substantial number of appeals were effectively denied a hearing because the complainant would be abroad but the tribunal in Britain. (An overseas service is now provided by a voluntary organisation, but it can barely cope with the volume of work.)

In January 1969 the Home Secretary ruled that Commonwealth citizens engaged to women living in Great Britain could not enter to marry and settle. The woman must leave the country and live with her husband. At the time some people thought that this was to prevent bogus marriages being used as a way around the immigration restrictions. But the Home Office itself said that this was not the case. The ruling struck a cruel blow to Asian women in Britain, because it meant that in

36

order to marry, many of them would have to leave the country and perhaps never see their parents again. This is an acute problem amongst the religiously more orthodox, as the men are permitted to marry outside the faith but the women are not. Therefore women relied more on arranged marriages with men in India, Pakistan and East Africa. At one blow their futures were transformed by a ruling which can only be interpreted as simple malice against the coloured community. A Conservative MP and ex-minister has admitted to me in private that Callaghan's ruling was unnecessary and in his opinion motivated by spitefulness. In June 1974 Roy Jenkins lifted the ban after a sustained campaign in the press and in Parliament.

We have only a sad story so far. It is not the story of the development of 'immigration control' that the authorities would have us believe. It is the story of the erosion of the rights of countless citizens and the erection of the immigration colour bar. Ten years ago we discussed the black man as the welcome stranger in our midst and talked about ways to help him 'integrate'. Today the black man is a public enemy, lurking in every cross-Channel lorry, landing by night on southern beaches or at Heathrow with forged papers; he is the 'alien wedge' and we discuss how to keep him out and how to get rid of those already here.

If this is done in our name, then our politicians have a very low opinion of us. The arguments about numbers and social resources have been dropped and it is now assumed that Britain admits black people on the basis of what is politically acceptable. In other words politicians think there is a climate of public opinion which dictates how many coloured people may be admitted. This represents a degrading view of the British people as incapable of understanding the world about them and given to spasms of uncontrolled race hatred. Are we really like this?

If the answer appears to be 'yes', then we and those responsible for erecting the colour bar should ask about the effect of public debate and the manner of legislation on the hardening and polarising of public attitudes. If ministers reacted as if to an alarming and horrible threat, they cannot expect the public to react otherwise. Has this been the case in race relations? Has the way in which policy has been developed produced its own justification by racist measures producing a racist public?

The story so far may be sad for us. But for the black community it has been a tragedy without apparent end. The next chapter will deal with the problem of the victims.

3.

Keeping out blacks

*'If you don't show a good record in refusing people
it is thought you are not doing your job properly.'*

So far I have described international trends and the
development of national legislation without quoting any of the
people directly concerned. The *way* in which the law is applied
is very important for the person whom the law affects, and there
is considerable scope for differences in the way the law is
applied. The law may hardly be enforced at all, as in the case of
the Litter Act. It may be pursued with utmost rigour, as in
murder cases. The police may let a suspect off with a warning;
they may take him to the police station and rough him up or
treat him very politely and considerately while nevertheless
charging and questioning him.

It is significant that I have to introduce a description of
the effects of the immigration laws on black people in terms of
the *criminal* law. After all, it is no crime to come to Britain and
the vast majority of black immigrants who come to Britain are
entitled to do so. The immigration rules are difficult to apply
justly (a point which does not bother legislators who do not
have to do the job). So we might expect immigration officers to
give people the benefit of any doubt and to ease their passage
through the entry procedures. But, as I described in the previous chapter, political and public 'debate' on immigration has
suggested that we are somehow threatened by black immigration and that we need protecting from the entry of black
people.

This influences the way in which officials act on the laws
in deciding whether a person shall enter the country or not.
The immigration officer at the 'port of entry' is the black

immigrant's first contact with British officialdom; and the immigrant finds a situation in which immigration officers see themselves as defending Britain against a black enemy. An American or Australian is waved through the barrier with a glance at his passport, but a black person has to prove that he is entitled to enter.

In the words of an ex-immigration officer: 'With an Indian or a Pakistani you assume he's come to stay; with an American you assume – sometimes wrongly – that he's only here on a visit. The job was simply keeping out black immigrants.' The officer is only the front line in a chain of command that stretches right back to the Home Secretary, and all the officers can do is to express the will of their political masters – keeping the blacks out. In the words of a civil rights expert:

> Daily experience of casework showed quite clearly that whatever the government's intention, the policy was interpreted by immigration officials as a duty to stem the flow of coloured immigrants. This observation was confirmed publicly by immigration officers' open letter in support of Mr Powell.

To quote the ex-immigration officer again:

> The politics of the vast majority of immigration officers are right-wing. Most are quite honest about this. It is significant that many would deny that they are racist but would claim that their right-wing view of immigration has been crystallised through being exposed to the country's immigrants at the port of entry. It disturbed me that in a group of men of above average intelligence there was such support for the views of Enoch Powell, especially since the statistical basis on which much of Powell's argument is founded could easily have been refuted by the information at their fingertips. Also interesting is the fact that many of my ex-colleagues were heavy off-duty drinkers. A number of reasons perhaps for this, the most important being first the tradition of the job – a throwback from service or colonial days – and second the pressures of the job itself.

So the black immigrant's first contact with the British is through an immigration officer who is doing an extraordinarily difficult job – almost impossible to do in any 'rational' way as we will see later – who is also likely to have strong right-wing views and to see his job as to protect Britain from the blacks.

Immigrants are subjected to lengthy interrogation at London Airport. After a long journey – perhaps the first one outside a village or small town – members of the family are separated and interviewed individually. Meanwhile relatives waiting to meet the new arrivals may also be interviewed and the police asked to investigate the home circumstances of the relatives in Britain.

Take the case of a wife joining her husband in Britain, together with their child. The husband will be asked the dates of birth of all his children, his wife's birthday and perhaps her sister's birthday. The child may then be asked the same questions and the wife similarly quizzed about her children, sisters and in-laws. A discrepancy in any detail can be sufficient to 'prove' that someone is lying. And yet in India and Pakistan birthdays are not remembered or celebrated and birth certificates are often not issued. The persons interrogated are also answering questions about this under considerable stress and might easily give a wrong or misleading answer when they know the facts quite well.

Ann Dummett describes a little boy and his father on opposite sides of the barrier, being asked about the cattle on the farm at home. How could the father know if a cow had died or another been bought or sold in the previous week? Moreover the boy was only twelve and came from a small village.

> Here he was in a nightmare world of glass and leather and plastic, being questioned over and over again by strangers who could not speak clearly enough for him to follow, and whose tone of voice was hectoring and hostile . . . his father was being kept away from him, but if only he could answer the question . . . he would get a chance to speak to his father.

41

The boy was sent back because it was said he was not really his father's son. The money carefully saved for the fare was lost, the hopes and ambitions of a family destroyed.

Perhaps the best known case of a confused little boy being sent home was Khadan Khan, who arrived earlier than expected and was not met. His bad English caused him to give the wrong address of his destination – Amberley Street instead of Emily Street.

In the words of the ex-immigration officer: 'If an officer really wants to keep someone out he can apply pressure – extensive and protracted questioning, leaving him to wait for a long time and so on.'

But supposing the immigrant has all the necessary documents – including the mandatory entry certificate?

> The youth behind the immigration desk acts on three basic assumptions. All black Commonwealth visitors are immigrants. Their passports are probably forged. And finally, visas supplied by Her Majesty's diplomats abroad are only an amusing irrelevancy.

For example an entry certificate is no guarantee of entry:

> A boy was to join his brother in England, but police reported that the house which he proposed to live in with his brother was grossly overcrowded. The brother immediately offered to put the boy with an uncle who had a house of his own and for whose respectability a British solicitor vouched. This offer, however, was refused on the grounds that there was no reason to believe that the boy would stay in the uncle's house and not subsequently move into the house where his brother was living.

Marriage certificates may not be accepted as genuine:

> A Pakistani woman's appeal to join a man she claims is her husband has been turned down . . . an adjudicator . . . said he was not satisfied that the couple were in fact married. The Wolverhampton Pakistan Muslim Welfare Association says that a marriage certificate produced was genuine.

Members of Parliament were told of a case of a fiancée refused admission to marry. The immigration officers checking her story asked to see letters from her future husband and came to the conclusion that the letters were not loving enough for the couple to be intending to get married. The old also suffer. Many frail old men trying to join their children who have settled in England have been interrogated, told they were not as old as they claimed and put on a plane home.

The immigration authorities are very tough with black students and from time to time refuse entry to students who have been accepted for courses on the grounds that they are not adequately qualified for the course. Many immigration officers may have two A levels, but does that qualify them as academic experts?

> A 22-year-old Pakistani whose brother in Rochdale has paid £260 in fees at a London computer training centre has been refused entry into this country. Three High Court judges upheld an immigration officer's decision that G.Sarwar was not geniune in making the course his primary reason for coming.

The *Guardian* reported in June 1973:

> Miss Khan arrived at Gatwick with an entry certificate issued to her in Guyana. She intended to take a fulltime one-year hairdressing course. The immigration officer considered that Miss Khan did not intend to return to Guyana on completion of her course, so her reason for coming to Britain was to settle. Undoubtedly Miss Kahn genuinely intended to take the course.

Miss Khan was refused entry. So even if black Commonwealth citizens have the proper documents they might be refused entry on the grounds that they might want to do something else at some other time.

This kind of attitude is seen very clearly in situations where Commonwealth citizens are trying to enter Britain for reasons other than to settle.

Three Pakistanis who flew over 4,000 miles to attend a relative's wedding in Manchester were detained at Heathrow Airport, held for six days, refused entry and flown back to Pakistan. They did not have entry certificates, which are not needed by visitors who satisfy the authorities that they have money and accommodation. The group had return tickets but not much cash and the Home Office said that the immigration authorities were not satisfied that they were only visitors. The bridegroom's brother said that his relatives had only intended to visit and that the incident had cost him nearly £2,000 in fares and legal fees. He had offered a security of £100,000 on their behalf.

The first two appeals heard against refusal of entry concerned visitors. The first was a Guyanese boy with a return ticket who, it was suggested, might find a suitable education course and then apply to the Home Office to stay, as he was perfectly entitled to do, since there is nothing illegal in applying for an alteration of conditions of entry, although most coloured Commonwealth immigrants will be told to go home to apply for a change of conditions. The second case involved a young man who had worked and saved over £200 for the return fare from St. Helena in order to have a holiday with his father in England. Both were refused entry; the second boy did not even see his father.

The fact that a visitor has relatives in the country already (surely the reason for his visit?) has been used as evidence that the visitor really intends to settle. One implication of this is that the black population may be largely deprived of the pleasure of welcoming friends and relatives from the home country. The tighter regulations also make it more risky to leave the country, so that black citizens become virtual prisoners once they have settled in Britain.

Even holiday-makers are at risk:

A Pakistani who had lived in Britain for six years was held as a suspected illegal immigrant after a weekend trip to Paris, although he carried a letter from his boss saying he was a *bona fide* employee. The Home Office said his passport did not appear to be in order.

A West Indian who has lived in Britain for eleven years was refused re-entry when he returned from a two-week course in Spain, as his passport is not stamped with a landing mark. He has been given a month in which to prove that he is a British resident before being deported.

Even black children visiting the continent on organised school parties run into difficulties; European officials are reluctant to admit them because they know the difficulties of re-entering Britain for a black child.

White Commonwealth holidaymakers (including those on a 'working holiday'), students and visitors have no problem of entry and re-entry. They are hardly ever aware that the Commonwealth Immigration Act applies to them; they change their terms of entry with ease – if they bother at all.

Officials at ports of entry, especially Heathrow, have a difficult job, because when the law divides families by, for example, not allowing Indian girls of 18 to join their parents, there is a great temptation to break the law. Unjust laws do not command respect. Additionally the documentation available to intending entrants may be sparse or unreliable, and when there is a high premium in avoiding the restrictions some forged documents are bound to be in circulation. Officials are therefore bound at times to be a little rough and arbitrary in their judgements. There is no way in which an unjust law can be made to work pleasantly.

Nonetheless this does not excuse harassment and violence. (A social worker once described to me how she had to protect a black person from physical assault by an official at Heathrow.) Some of the techniques adopted to resolve uncertainties are on the borderline that divides administrative procedures from harassing and punitive tactics. Sometimes X-rays are used to judge the age of a child because a child over 16 is not allowed to join his parents in the UK. (Until 1972 aliens could be joined by children up to the age of 21.) The X-ray technique is very unreliable for this purpose, giving anything up to two years' error in assessing actual age. Thus a boy of 14 might be excluded, while it is unlikely but possible that a boy of 18 would be admitted. In fact it is unsafe to try and bring a child into the country over the age of 12. There have been cases when delays in admitting children have resulted in them passing the age of eligibility before their cases have been processed. This is especially a problem when queues or quotas are enforced.

The internal examination of women and girls to see if they are mothers or virgins is plainly a method which frightens, degrades and shocks the women concerned. Checking for virginity is very unreliable, but such checks have actually led to parents disowning a daughter who they thought had dishonoured them because the medical report was that the girl was not a virgin. The idea of this test is to see whether a girl claiming to be an unmarried daughter is, in fact, unmarried. Such practices have continued at Heathrow in spite of Home Office denials.

Immigrants held pending further enquiries or appeals are held in custody by Securicor, a private security agency. The ex-immigration officer again:

> If you are looking for the real racists, look at some of the Securicor people. We'd phone up the detention centre and one of their people would come over. 'Right, Sambo (or Abdul),' he'd say, 'Where's your bloody bag?' Once I had to go over to the centre to re-interview someone. The place stank, there was screaming and shouting going on everywhere. There seemed to be no proper records kept of who was sent to the centre, and it took them a long time to find the man I'd gone to see. Securicor are licensed by the Home Office to guard the detainees, but we're not able to tell them how they should do the job. When I got back I made a complaint. I was regarded as a bit odd because of my attitudes.

Other detainees are sent to prison and many remain there for many months; there is a special wing for such cases at

Pentonville Prison. Many of the prisoners have committed no offence and have been charged with none, yet they remain in custody for months. Those appealing against refusal of admission have not 'landed' and therefore officially do not exist. The harshness of the regulations and the rigour with which they are applied can mean that those contesting refusal of admission can have their agony prolonged as friends and well-wishers make repeated attempts to have decisions reversed – a hopeless task in a situation where the government is determined to keep out blacks at all costs.

Even those who have committed an offence may fare worse than they might have expected, though the following case reported by the *Guardian* might be thought lucky:

> An Indian who was recommended for deportation spent four weeks in prison before it was discovered that he could not be deported as he had been in Britain for more than five years. The Home Office admitted that a mistake had been made, but said it took time for various documents to come from the police and the court for checking.

> *If tears can better explain my case than words*
> *I could only say that I and my family*
> *are actually crying when my friend is typing*
> *this letter to you for me.*

> *While I appreciate your difficulties, I regret to*
> *say your case is due for further consideration*
> *and . . . I can offer no indication of the*
> *eventual date of issue of your voucher.*

The immigration officer is the agent of the government, and the government is committed to keeping blacks out. But it is not just the government and immigration officials; diplomatic agencies also operate in the same way. No clearer example of the way in which these three operate can be found than the case of the East African Asians.

Towards the end of the 1960s the African governments began to squeeze the non-citizen Asians out by denying them trading licences (or granting only temporary licences) and Africanising many sectors of the public service. It was for such a situation that the Asians had chosen their citizenship and for which Britain had apparently offered it. But the inflow of Asians was stopped by the 1968 Immigration Act.

> Callaghan, indeed, in introducing the 1968 Bill spoke of the 'solemn obligation' which the Bill was violating; he could hardly have conveyed more clearly that he considered any dishonour preferable to the presence of a few thousand more people of dark skins.

What were the Asians to do ? Here are some extracts from a report on their situation in East Africa:

> British citizens are also confused about who issues the vouchers. The British High Commission writes to the applicants saying they are 'waiting to hear from my issuing authorities' and so on. On the other hand, if someone writes to the Home Office, they reply that it is a matter for the High Commission. Recently, a further complication has been added and people are now being referred by the Home Office to the Migration and Visa Department of the Foreign Office.

> It is not possible to describe the atmosphere of hopelessness and insecurity that prevails amongst the British Asian community today. The visible signs of their miserable existence – the one room shared by as many as eight people, the 'borrowing' of a few shillings to buy flour, the children poorly clad and out of school.

> But this is not all. Many actually fear arrest and imprisonment.

> The British government has only been able to avoid actual starvation amongst the unemployed because it has been able to exploit Asian family solidarity and community loyalty . . . There are cases, for instance, where one member of the family who has Ugandan citizenship or a work permit has been supporting as many as eight people on his wage.

> These people have been crushed and humiliated and it is inevitable that when they do reach Britain the children in

particular are going to take a long time working out their problems before they are able to settle down.

One man aged 44, who had been unemployed and destitute for months, brought his 18-year-old son in for interview, saying that he knew that he personally was 'finished', but adding: 'For God's sake, do something for my son'.

It is a terrifying thought that once here (in the UK) the children who have already suffered so much may be referred to as an 'influx' and a 'problem' by unthinking people, giving them a permanent sense of inferiority.

Some of the children were unlikely to come at all because they believed they were on the waiting list for vouchers as dependant children, but while waiting passed the qualifying age for children and later discovered that they had not made proper formal application. Some social workers believe the British government hoped that this would deter the parents from coming to the UK as they would be unwilling to part from their children.

What were these British citizens to do, sitting on packed suitcases for months on end, the children's schooling completely stopped, money running out and a government anxious to see them out of the country? Some decided to take a chance and make for Britain, the country of which they were citizens and whose passport they held. But they set off without the appropriate documents. The British government was determined not to let them in. But they had nowhere else to go as they were not citizens of any other country – certainly not of the East African states they had left. To return a citizen to a country from which he started is a pointless but punitive operation. He may be redeported straight back to the UK, or he may be beginning a very much longer trip. Punitive measures were adopted, resulting in the creation of the so-called 'shuttlecocks'.

Ten who left Entebbe on 1 June (1970) were turned back at the Austrian border. They arrived in Athens with tickets for Hamburg but were told by Greek authorities that they could not stay in Greece and were flown to Belgrade. They had booked into a hotel, little knowing that they would later have cause to regret this as they spent most of their money on accommodation. They flew to West Germany but were returned to Belgrade where they stayed in waiting rooms. For three days they had no food. One of the group wrote: 'We went to the British Embassy and told them every trouble and told them to help us. But they never gave a single answer'.

Another couple with a small baby were in a group of 16 who obtained tickets to Heathrow, where they were refused admission. In spite of the intervention of the relatives of the couple with the baby, they were all deported back to Belgrade. This group also ran out of funds and wrote on 9 June: 'We are sorry to inform you that we have not taken any piece of food for the last three days. We sleep on the benches in the airport'.

One passenger went even further, as he was put back on the plane in which he had arrived from East Africa; he went to Burundi, Rwanda, South Africa, Mauritius and Sydney.

He then came all the way back again having spent over sixty hours in the air. When he got back to Heathrow he was promptly put into Ashford Remand Centre. By that time he was completely disoriented and did not know what the date or day of the week was.

RVK came to Britain via Holland. From Harwich he was sent back to the Hook, where he was kept in detention for several days. He was then deported back to Britain. From Harwich he was taken to Heathrow and deported to Entebbe, where he was refused admission. He was taken on to Nairobi and then deported back to Heathrow via Entebbe. From Heathrow he was returned to Pentonville Prison.

Again it must be emphasised that each time a person is deported the British authorities are well aware of the fact that he will come back again.

The ex-immigration officer:

They'd be sent back to East Africa three times, then – after spending days in a plane and in airport lounges, with only a few shillings – they'd be allowed in and sent to Pentonville for three weeks. After that they'd be admitted for three months, a period usually extended by three months by the Home Office. This process was intended to deter the African countries from decanting their Asian population on to Britain.

One way in which this traffic in human cargo was reduced was the government's use of diplomatic channels to persuade many countries not to admit British passport holders from ex-colonies unless they had entry certificates for Britain. Other kinds of pressure was applied to airlines to discourage them from carrying such passengers.

The political intention behind these activities could be seen in the sharp deterioration in the handling of British Asians in the run-up to the 1970 and 1974 general elections. During these periods deportation went ahead ruthlessly without any consideration being given to compassionate cases or cases of extreme hardship, as had been the practice before.

At the time of the expulsion of Asian British citizens from Uganda, the British government acted immediately to block the possible entry routes to the UK. There was considerable confusion because some Asians had failed to get Ugandan citizenship but could no longer prove their British nationality. Others were less able to prove they were British – deserted or divorced wives for example. (In one case a deserted mother was offered entry without her child because the child was on the passport of the runaway father.) It was a crisis in which it was necessary to cut corners in order to save lives. But it was widely observed that the High Commission in Kampala was delaying or denying many who had a right to come to Britain – there was certainly no sense of urgency and it may have cost some people their lives. An eye-witness in Kampala gave me many examples of the ways in which husbands and wives were separated and children sent to different countries from one or both parents. Hundreds, perhaps thousands, vanished without trace.

Many Asians were made stateless during the Ugandan crisis, some are trying to make a life for themselves in Europe after spending time in a refugee camp. Their statelessness arose from confusions surrounding the renunciation of British citizenship: on taking Ugandan citizenship the applicant had to renounce British citizenship, but there was a period of grace – three months – during which he could reclaim it. The three months were calculated from the date of the receipt of a letter reminding the applicant that the final renunciation was due. This could be two months, or very much longer, after the initial application. During the crisis the Ugandan government said that it would only accept renunciations made within three months of the original application and the British government also reverted to a three months rule, not allowing citizenship to be claimed back after three months from application. This created considerable confusion and many found that they had not gained Ugandan citizenship and could not get their British citizenship back again.

We need to think very calmly about all this. The people who are harassed at Heathrow or sent like so much luggage around the world on pointless journeys are ordinary people like us. Young wives with their husbands and small children; students full of hope for the future; old people looking forward to a restful retirement; businessmen, workers, housewives, technicians, secretaries, schoolchildren, craftsmen and clerks. Just ordinary people.

But once people are treated as a problem they are no longer treated as people. Close your eyes and think of your little son, whom you have waited three years to see, being questioned on the other side of a barrier and then tearfully being put onto an aeroplane for the other side of the world. Think of your wife and yourself, seeing friends and relatives waiting, being turned back with your crying baby to make yet another ten-hour jet trip to nowhere. Think of a student joining her parents and little brother, turned back at Heathrow and sent to live in Bombay with an aged aunt she hardly knows. And if you dare, think of all those photographs you have seen of Jewish families and little children taken in the war. Can such horrors happen here?

Once you have embarked upon the course described in the last chapter, all the misery and suffering, all the degradation of the oppressed and the oppressor is possible. Need one ask why so little of all this is reported and discussed in the newspapers or on television?

Just as the numbers game leads to questions about the people already here, so the kind of outlook we have seen in the treatment of black immigrants spreads to those already here. Illegal immigrants have been seen as a major problem (in fact there are probably not very many) and the police now have a special section to deal with this – just as they are to have a special section to deal with pickets. Black people involved in motoring incidents are now asked for their passports as well as their driving licences.

It has been common for the police to raid houses at night to check for illegal immigrants; the 'midnight knock' is a reality for many people in Britain. In some towns policemen have been given medals for their work in tracking down illegal immigrants.

The retrospective nature of the 1971 Act removed protection from illegal or irregular immigrants already openly living here. In spite of promises that there would be no witch hunts, the police still search whole streets, blocks and workplaces and require all coloured people to prove their right to be here.

There are now cases of people being picked up at work in their working clothes and deported without relatives or friends knowing what has happened to them. There can be no appeal because officially the immigrant has not 'landed' – he was not here at all.

The policing of black immigrants spreads wider; some hospitals are asked to check the credentials of their employees; schools may be asked to check parents' passports; the Social Security office may also check passports or pass personal details to the Home Office.

In April 1974 Roy Jenkins declared an amnesty for all illegal immigrants who came to Britain before 1 January 1973. The amnesty was strictly for *illegal* immigrants only; in other words it applied to people who entered without going through passport control when they were subject to control. It did not cover people who were overstaying conditional entry or who were in any way in Britain in breach of their terms of entry. Thus of the first 90 cases examined by the Home Office after the amnesty, 69 were not covered by the amnesty and were therefore liable to deportation. This led to some loss of confidence in the amnesty itself.

The amnesty and the lifting of the Callaghan ban can be effected without legislation. A future Home Secretary can declare the amnesty to be at an end and can change the immigration rules to exclude husbands and fiancés. It should not be thought that Roy Jenkins was being generous in lifting the husbands' ban; he did so only after he assured himself that there would not be a 'new wave of colonial immigrants from the Indian sub-continent'. In other words he accepts the numbers and blacks-are-a-problem argument; and in changing the rules he maintained the privileges of EEC citizens by allowing them to bring in dependant children over the age of 21 – a right no longer enjoyed by Commonwealth citizens. These changes were accomplished without any marked protest or political 'row' in spite of the attitudes adopted by the right wing.

Immigration is no longer a problem of integration, but of 'law and order' or 'keeping them out at all costs'. If Chapter 2 was a sad story, this chapter has been a horror story. It has not been told to send cold shivers down your spine but to show what can happen to people once others call them a problem.

If you agreed with Harold Wilson in 1965 you can really have no objection to anything that has been described.

Lie in bed at night and think of the anguish and bewilderment of British families wilfully and deliberately broken up; think of your own family treated as unwanted luggage by others. Think of trying to understand men imposing such suffering on you and those you love because they refuse to see you as people and because they have power over you.

4.
The police and the courts

We have seen how the definition of the coloured person as 'a problem' influences the attitudes of the authorities against them. This is nowhere more clear than in the case of the police and the courts.

The police are involved with black people in a number of different ways: they are involved with immigration control, they also have contact with individual members of the black community settled in Britain, and as a 'force' they relate to the black community as a whole. In all these situations there is a high degree of conflict.

The police are contacted by the immigration authorities when enquiries are being made about the information given by intending immigrants and when information is required on the social circumstances in which the new migrant will be living. In these latter cases, are the police really the right people to deal with what look like social work or social welfare questions ? To ask this is merely to draw attention again to the extent to which the whole issue of coloured migration is treated as a police problem. For example, the police might be asked how many people live in a particular house. The answer they give may be the number of people who were in the house when the police last visited it (perhaps on an illegal immigrant hunt). Thus visitors from another town staying overnight or relations staying for a family celebration may be included among the residents of the house.

When the police visit in search of answers to questions like, 'Is this house overcrowded ?' they may find no one in and so ask a white neighbour about crowding. This sort of hearsay evidence can be used to exclude a child from Britain and his parents.

But it is in their pursuit of illegal or alleged illegal immigrants that the police come into severe conflict with the coloured population. The 'alleged' illegal immigrants are an important group of people; these are people who entered Britain before the tightening of the colour bar – East African Asians who came in before 1968, for example. But they also include others who in the days before black immigration became such a political issue came in either in irregular ways (for example, seamen jumping ship) or who just didn't get the right papers stamped. Such people – here quite legitimately – might find it extraordinarily difficult to *prove* their right to be here.

In spite of promises from the Home Secretary, 'witch hunts' did take place against illegal immigrants. In fact the promise given by Carr was a silly one because you can not enact a law and then ask the police not to enforce it. One commentator has said that 114 people were detained between January and November 1973; 86 were deported and only 14 released. (What has happened to the other 14?) This figure may suggest a high proportion of illegal immigrants, but the figures are misleading, because once the retrospective law came into effect many people who were known to have entered illegally but who had survived the period in which they could previously have been deported, suddenly became eligible for deportation again. Some of these were known to the police because they had asked for help and the police had advised them on how to regularise their situation.

When they 'go fishing' the police have much less luck. In one day during a series of raids in London late in 1973 the police visited ten different premises, detained fourteen people and later released ten – although other immigrants say that between 35 and 50 were picked up. Raids have taken place in London, Dartford, Southall, Bishop's Stortford, Hitchin and Bradford, and perhaps in many other places. Immigrants can be held 'on suspicion' for an unlimited period. Here are some examples of raids in London:

> 62-year-old Kadar Meah, a British citizen who fought in the Second World War as a merchant seaman and took British citizenship because he thought Britain 'a civilised place', was confined to his room for two hours while police went through everything he possessed. The first time in 32 years of residence in this country that Mr Meah has had serious dealings with the British police and the only trouble after a life of travelling the world.

A West-End cook 'was sound asleep when police entered his room at 7.30 in the morning'. Together with two friends he was 'detained in his bed for two hours', his room searched and his personal possessions scattered; the men were insulted and abused by the police, who did not show warrants and who searched private documents and mail.

The searching of private papers is especially sinister. This is a practice that was developed by the drug and bomb squads. By noting names and addresses in letters, address books and other papers it is possible, with the use of computers and information from passports, National Insurance cards and the Department of Health and Social Security, to build up a detailed picture of the whole coloured population in Britain.

The police do not operate by raids alone. There is a report of a woman asking a policeman the way; she was taken to a police station and held until her passport was brought in. An Indian teacher had a class interrupted by police who had been told that he was an illegal immigrant. A 25-year-old Indian wrestler was jailed for three months after a Special Branch raid. He had a wife and child dependant on him. He was freed without being convicted.

Here is the case of ARM, a 26-year-old factory worker from Pakistan. He has worked here five years and has applied to be naturalised:

> The police came to my work and said they wanted me to help them with enquiries. I was taken to Southall police station and they said: 'You are an illegal immigrant.'

> When I said no, they started hitting me and said they
> would stop hitting me if I would say yes. Sometimes they
> were hitting me on my knees with a truncheon, some-
> times on my back or banging my head against the wall.
> They had their hands over my eyes while they were hit-
> ting me so I couldn't identify them. One policeman
> would stand on my feet while another hit me. Many times
> they did this. One I could smell alcohol on his breath.

The police had been to a CID party. ARM obtained the
services of a lawyer and had medical evidence of injuries which
supported his story. A week later, he was taken from work to
Southall police station again and from there to Heathrow. The
police hoped for a quick deportation but were thwarted by the
High Court granting bail. Four days after arriving at Heathrow
he was free. What redress would ARM have had and how
would he have sought it if he had found himself in Pakistan
with no money? The police know the answer to that question.

The idea that our policemen are wonderful, but there
are a few 'bad apples' in the barrel, clearly will not hold water
in the situation I am describing. The police are actually in
conflict with the black community, and like the immigration
officer the policeman sees himself in the front line of defence
against the blacks. So when a policeman kicks a door down and
bursts into an immigrant home he is only doing what James
Callaghan or Robert Carr did on the national level with legislation and regulations.

When the police are carrying out their general duties,
here again conflict seems to be general and typical between them
and the black population, although some districts and some
police stations receive more publicity than others: Hands-
worth, Lewisham, Ladywell, Southall, Division X, and the
Special Patrol Group (who have to date killed two people –
both Pakistani boys armed with toy guns).

How does the police force care for the black community?
The National Council for Civil Liberties submitted a memor-
andum to the Select Committee on Race Relations and Immigration, in which they said: 'We would be failing in our duty if

we omitted to convey our considered opinion that the worsening situation between the police and the black community is very serious indeed.' The section which follows examines firstly the relation between the police and black *communities* and secondly that between the police and individual members of the black community.

In 1970 the practice of 'Paki-bashing' hit the newspaper headlines. Groups of white youths (skinheads) in London were prowling after dark and attacking, beating and robbing lone Asians, many of whom, working in restaurants and hospitals, had to return from work after dark. One Muslim community leader had a dossier of 36 attacks, 27 involving physical injury and 19 requiring hospital treatment, which included stitching in six cases and two weeks in hospital for another. In 22 of the cases the police were notified, but no arrests were made and nothing more was heard. In the other 14 cases victims said that they wished to avoid trouble, or didn't think the police would be interested.

The police are, of course, unable to solve all cases. Swift attacks by night are over before the police arrive and arrests are unlikely. But sometimes there are witnesses:

Mr Ali was attacked by six youths and required two stitches for a head injury. He managed to apprehend one of the boys whom he could obviously recognise again. An Englishman who was standing at the bus stop came to Mr Ali and told him to release the boy, which he did. When the police came, Mr Ali pointed out the Englishman and told the police to take a statement from him, but they did nothing. Nothing has been heard from the police since.

In the Euston and King's Cross area over 30 cases were documented in detail, involving over 50 Pakistanis in 1967. The police made no arrests and asked one victim: 'Why didn't you catch them?' One white man was caught when two beat up an Asian. He was handed over to the police at Tottenham Court Road police station and six witnesses came forward from the public. The other attacker was never caught and the case against the one caught was dismissed for lack of evidence at the Old Bailey three months later. The police had not bothered to contact the witnesses.

The culmination of these attacks was the murder of Tosir Ali. He was done to death outside his house in Tower Hamlets. His throat was cut. The police seemed unable to find the culprit and even put around the story that there were a lot of Asians attacking one another. In a television programme on the subject of Paki-bashing a Pakistani worker showed his wounds from a recent attack and said he had identified his attackers but the police had done nothing. The next day he was arrested, taken to Leman Street police station. Here he said he was abused, slapped and accused of murdering Tosir Ali. He was released after seven hours in custody. Complaints were made to the Home Office; nearly five months later the Home Office reported that the findings of an enquiry had been sent to the Director of Public Prosecutions. The DPP said there was insufficient evidence to prosecute the officers concerned.

Eventually two white youths were tried for the murder. There was insufficient evidence to convict one and the other youth pleaded guilty to manslaughter.

The Asian communities affected decided that they must protect themselves. In the Euston–King's Cross area Asian patrols succeeded in reducing attacks. But soon the Asians found *themselves* being apprehended on offensive weapons charges. Now this is quite correct in law; you may not carry a weapon to defend yourself. But what was the Asian population to do when it looked as if the police were not interested in protecting them and then would not let them protect themselves in the way they thought best?

One Pakistani heard a friend being attacked and rushed into the street to help – he had been stirring curry when he heard the cries and had the spoon in his hand when he came on to the street. He was charged with having an offensive weapon. The police had denied that skinheads went out looking for Asians to bash. When the Asians took defensive action, however, the police spoke of 'civil war' and greater friction 'between the two factions'.

So the Asians had been told to catch their attackers and when they did the police failed to prosecute seriously; they were told to stand up for themselves and when they did they finished up in court on charges themselves.

Of course we have to understand both what is actually going on in police-immigrant relations and what both sides *believe* to be going on. The police are often inexcusably ill-informed about the way of life and community organisation of the various immigrant groups. This, plus verbal abuse from a few policemen, can provoke hostile reaction from the black community which in itself seems to justify police attitudes. Once the local community has lost confidence in the police it will act as if the police cannot be trusted and will interpret all police action as hostile. But how can mutual mistrust and hostility be avoided in the climate I have described? The police would need to renounce their political masters for things to be significantly changed.

Here are some cases that look like police aggression against the black community.

The Mangrove restaurant in Notting Hill was a community centre for West Indians. It was raided three times by the police in search of drugs. They never found any. Eventually a demonstration was held to protest against this treatment. A noisy but peaceful demonstration of about 150 people marched around Notting Hill and North Paddington. In Portnall Road a melée occurred in which 24 police officers were hurt. Nine blacks appeared at the Old Bailey after 18 had come before the Marylebone magistrates. The charges included riotous assembly, affray, grievous bodily harm, offensive weapons, actual bodily harm and wounding. The riot charges were dismissed by the magistrates but reimposed at the Old Bailey.

It emerged from the evidence that the police had a plain-clothes photographer in an unmarked van covering the demonstration and that charges were brought against people identified from photographs. About 500 policemen were on duty against the demonstrators and policemen left their bus with truncheons drawn. The demonstrators retaliated although their 'offensive weapons' consisted mainly of placards. Only one policeman was prepared to say that the events constituted a riot and he also stated that the Mangrove restaurant was 'a haunt for prostitutes, criminals and ponces'. The whole affair looked more like a police attack on the demonstration. Five of the defendants were acquitted on all charges; out of 22 charges against the nine, only seven minor counts were proved against four of them.

These events were very dramatic, but only the culmination of a long history of harassment by the police. The manager of the Mangrove speaks:

> Besides the raids, there've been other visits, and people on their way home from here have been stopped and questioned: 'Have you come from the Mangrove? What's going on there? What are you carrying?' And because of the way the searches are carried out I've lost a lot of custom: people don't like being lined up against a wall, having flashlights shone over them, when they've come here for a meal.

Other restaurants and clubs as well as private parties have been persistently raided by the police. One visit by the Special Patrol Group to the Metro Youth Club in search of two black youths resulted in a fight. The outcome was the appearance in court of four West Indians on 21 charges ranging from affray (almost as serious as treason) to offensive weapons. All were acquitted on all charges after the jury had been out for 30 minutes. They plainly rejected the police evidence.

Do the police have any particular grievance against the black population? The Manchester Community Relations Committee said that most trainee policemen were prejudiced. 'They are inclined to believe that immigrants are more criminal than the population at large, whereas they are not, according to Manchester and Salford records. When presented with their own official evidence, by their own officers, trainees have refused to believe it.' The black population is also thought to be connected with special kinds of crime: in the 1950s and early 1960s it was living off immoral earnings, then they became drug pushers, and now 'mugging' is the main crime of which blacks are accused. These are all stereotypes bearing little relation to actual evidence, but they do give some idea of the attitudes adopted by the police. The Police Federation's own evidence to the Select Committee on Immigration and Police relations suggest ill-informed and derogatory attitudes towards the black community, its organisation and leaders.

The main complaints against the police are of general harassment, refusal to act when a complaint about a crime is made, unreasonable searching and questioning; verbal abuse; physical assault; fabrication of evidence and charges out of proportion to the offence; improper attempts to prevent bail and breaches of the Judge's Rules. If such complaints were based on one or two cases only we might attribute them to misunderstanding or inexperience on either side. But the continuous and systematic nature of these complaints points to something not only more serious, but *entirely expected*, given the definition of the black man as a public enemy.

A few individual cases:

Mr Colin Stevenson is a railway porter. He is black. Some weeks ago two young men were making a nuisance of themselves on the platform of Richmond Station. While someone in the station office called the police, Mr Stevenson went to restrain the men. On the platform opposite stood Mr Maurice of Putney. He saw Stevenson check the men and heard them offer him a selection of 'nigger' style insults while they prepared to attack him. Mr Stevenson picked up a destination board to defend himself.

'I thought Stevenson would have been quite justified in hitting them, but he didn't,' said Maurice.

At this moment the police arrived. 'Stevenson went towards the police,' Maurice continued, 'and I thought he was going to help them. But they lost interest in the young men, tore the board out of Stevenson's hand and hit him over the head with it. A policeman took out a truncheon and hit Stevenson on the head and shoulders, while a police sergeant handcuffed him. Stevenson offered no violence. I went over and offered my name and address as a witness.' Asked why he neglected Mr Maurice's offer, the sergeant said: 'I didn't think it was relevant.' He added that Stevenson appeared to go 'berserk' when the police arrived.

The magistrate dismissed the charges against Stevenson but awarded no costs against the police.

Satram Kane was accused of stealing £50 from his employer. He appeared before the magistrate the next day and pleaded guilty. Asked why he had got into trouble like this Kane said he hadn't; his confession was untrue and forced from him. Kane claims that in the police station he was slapped around the face and told that his wife and mother would be involved in the case if he didn't confess – so he confessed. Then the employer found the 'stolen' money at the back of a drawer. Satram Kane had been made to confess to a crime that never took place.

The case was sent to the DPP and raised with the Home Office, but there was deemed to be insufficient evidence to take any action. The fact that complaints about police behaviour are dealt with privately and internally by the police themselves does not encourage confidence in their findings.

There are continuous complaints from black youths that drugs are planted on them; this ensures that at least one charge can be brought against them when picked up. One important implication of bringing drugs charges or using affray and riot charges for minor brawls is that such offences if proved can carry deportation in addition to any other sentences. Thus the police may be tempted to promote their immigration control and 'public protection' policy in this way. The police also seem to overreact to incidents involving black people. Thus a constable approaching a group of loitering youths may radio for help, and the arrival of police cars and more constables results in a crowd gathering, jostling and arguments – and charges. In fact these situations look very much like police riots. The best we can say about these situations is that the arrival of the police in force is itself highly provocative.

The best-known case of this was the 'battle of Atlantic Road'. A Nigerian diplomat parked his car on double yellow lines. When he came back to his car he was dragged out and hustled off to Brixton police station. The incident drew a crowd and police reinforcements were sent for. The police seemed to grab people at random from the crowd – people were held by the neck, thrown into police vans and beaten in the vans. In court a number of independent witnesses supported the claim that black bystanders had been grabbed for no apparent reason. One man, having seen the incident, went into a shop; when he came out a policeman shouted 'There's one here,' and hit him with his truncheon, fracturing his arm in three places. The constable concerned, according to the victim, said that if the injured man said in court that he'd had an accident at work, charges against him of possessing an offensive weapon would be dropped.

No independent witnesses were produced to support the police story. But what happened in court will be described later.

The latest harassing tactic is known as 'sussing' – picking people up 'on suspicion'. Thus youths can be arrested because, in the opinion of a police officer, they are acting *as if* they are committing or about to commit a crime. There are no victims, no witnesses – just the police against the accused.

A typical suss case would involve bringing youths before the court and saying that two police officers saw the accused walking in a crowded street and touching people's handbags and coats, as if they were going to steal. It might even be said that they looked into the shopping-bag of a woman wearing a blue coat and grey slacks – but the woman is not produced in court. The fact that the accused was said to be looking into cars might also make him 'a suspicious person'. How can one answer such charges except by denying the policeman's story?

'Loitering with intent' is another unanswerable charge to which black citizens feel themselves to be especially prone. 'As soon as DH left the underground station he was seized by a man who produced a police identity card and demanded to search him. He was hustled into a shop doorway where the policeman was joined by others. The officer said that he had been seen to jostle a woman, reach into her handbag and attempt to steal her purse.' DH offered to go to the police station to be searched there. The search was thorough but revealed nothing. He was put in a cell and bailed out at 12.30 pm. He pleaded not guilty and the magistrates put him on bail on condition that he report to the police station every morning. As a trainee nurse on shift work, DH could only report in the afternoon; he did so for a week. The second week he was put back in a cell and then into a remand home for breaking bail. He was in custody for two weeks before being bailed again.

At Marlborough Street Court DH got three months imprisonment for stealing goods which were never produced from a victim who was never identified. He lost his job as a trainee nurse.

The 'Oval case' formed part of the evidence for complaints by West Indian youths that they were being habitually picked on by the transport police. Four black men came out of the Oval tube station and were stopped by plain-clothes police: 'Some of you blokes have been going around nicking handbags and we are going to search you.' A scuffle broke out and more plain-clothes men joined in. One man got away but was later picked up with the help of a police dog. They claim they were beaten and abused at Kennington Road police station and attempts were made to obtain false confessions from them. Seventeen charges were brought against the four and the only witnesses produced were for the defence.

The 'sussing' and harassing of black youth on the streets and in their clubs and cafés seems to be increasing. This increase parallels the rise of the 'unemployed black youth problem'. Many young black men are unwilling to take what they see as the menial jobs, serving the white community, that satisfied their parents. They know also that they will be discriminated against in seeking other jobs. So for better or worse some choose not to work. It is against this kind of youth that police effort seems to be directed. It is widely felt amongst the more politically-minded members of the black population that this is an effort to force young men into work. Thus individuals and institutions (cafés, gambling houses, parties etc) which do not conform to the local routine of work and controlled leisure are subject to attack. The idea seems to be to isolate those who will not conform and accept their low-grade position in society. They are isolated as criminals and singled out as a special threat to society.

The recent White Paper on Police/Immigrant Relations focused on the 'problem' of the international rebellion of black youth and the need to cajole or force them into work. A commentator on this question has observed that it was to enforce wage labour in the London docks in 1798 that the police force was first set up. The work that had to be done in the docks was the unloading of sugar produced by the black slaves in the West Indies.

In court, it looks as if, on balance, black citizens do not do too badly. There have been some significant acquittals by juries. But of course most cases are heard by magistrates, and with one or two exceptions magistrates seem to believe the police rather than the accused when there is a conflict of evidence.

The magistrate in the Atlantic Road case sentenced five of the six accused to custodial treatment (one sentence suspended). He also made a widely reported observation that after 150 years of maintaining order with good humour the Metropolitan Police were being obstructed and insulted by 'an element'.

The judge in the Oval case asked why the youths had not shouted for help or called the police when the plain-clothes men started pushing them around, and why did they not complain to the uniformed police about the brutal treatment they had received. In these cases the jury dismissed the seven charges for which the accused were meant to have confessed, but found them guilty on ten other charges including 'attempting to steal property from a person unknown' and assaulting the police. The youths had their appeals upheld, but no action was taken against the policemen who had arrested them.

Towards the end of 1973, six detectives from the drug drag squad were charged with conspiring to pervert the course of justice; they had been involved in a case in which police records have been 'doctored and monkeyed around with'. The case led to the quashing of sentences on a Pakistani family allegedly involved in drug smuggling. And in August 1974, Detective-Sergeant Grant Smith of Scotland Yard admitted planting evidence on suspects and obtaining three convictions, including that of a black student taking part in an anti-apartheid demonstration. Several enquiries are currently being conducted into police corruption; policemen whose evidence alone put men in jail have been suspended or dismissed, but most of their victims still lie in jail.

Recent changes in the regulations relating to jury service have brought more working-class people on to juries. This is because you now only need to be a voter and not a property-owner to serve on a jury. It may be a coincidence that this has been accompanied by some important jury acquittals, as in the Mangrove and Metro cases, which involved rejecting the evidence of policemen and believing the accused instead. It is much less likely to be a coincidence that Sir Robert Mark has attacked the jury system just at the point where the basis of jury service has been widened. Working-class people have a much less favourable opinion of the police and in some cases unhappy experience of police activity. Juries used to be made up entirely of the kind of people policemen addressed as 'Sir' or 'Madam' and so the police could be pretty sure of a more than fair hearing. However, the Lord Chancellor has now said that the occupations of jurors may not be divulged to the defence in a case. The prosecution is under no such restriction and will therefore be more able to get the kind of jury it wants.

Robert Mark also wishes to abolish the caution and reduce the scope of the Judges' Rules. It needs very little imagination to see what this could mean to the ignorant, the easily-intimidated or the non-English speaker.

Practice in courts varies from region to region and between judges and magistrates. Barristers appearing before certain judges know all the careful preparation of their case has been wasted. Appearing before other judges they know that all involved in the case will be treated with respect and consideration by the judge.

The law is no more above public opinion than it is above politics. So it is not surprising that some judges and magistrates believe that there are too many black people in Britain and that they are a special threat to the established social order. Perhaps the most blatant – and maybe unusual – case of prejudice was of a magistrate hearing formal application for bail. He asked the lawyer: 'Is your client black?' On being told he was, he replied: 'Then no bail.'

Another very serious incident involved a judge who joined prosecuting counsel in harassing an expert witness (a sociologist) who was testifying on mistaken identity in cases involving race. The defence had to withdraw this witness because the contempt with which he was being treated was damaging the defence case.

Some judges appear unable to resist references to the racial or national origin of defendants. Sentencing a Pakistani for fiddling his Social Security, Judge Mason said: 'It is high time you and your fellow-countrymen got it into your heads that we are not going to tolerate this sort of thing.' Why 'and your fellow-countrymen'?

The one area in which the courts can give free rein to prejudiced or other beliefs about black men is in their power of deportation. Thus, after serving a sentence, an offender may be expelled from the country as a further punishment. Recommendations are made at the discretion of the court.

In mid-1972, when 'mugging' was the current scare and three years' prison the average sentence (providing the victim wasn't badly hurt), three white men involved in beating a group of black men which resulted in one dying, received one year's imprisonment (suspended in one case). Need one ask why the black population think that the courts are against them as well as the police?

Finally, the courts can use the Mental Health Act to commit an offender to an institution. In some courts this seems to be used in order to secure custody of first offenders and others who would usually only be put on probation. A particularly unpleasant aspect of such cases is that the person involved may be allowed out under supervision and returned to custody without any further hearing. Such a case occurred in Manchester when a West Indian boy was released on condition that he lived with his mother. In fact he was on bad terms with his mother and soon left to stay with his girl friend. One day he was having a 'friendly' chat with a policeman outside the supermarket when this fact came out. A police car was called for and the boy found himself back in a mental hospital still clutching his groceries. It was forty-eight hours before his friends found him.

One scandalous practice that connects courts, police and lawyers is the offering of money (said to be about £40) to policemen for bringing legal aid cases to certain law firms. Black people are especially vulnerable to these latter-day bounty hunters. The firms do well from legal aid and welcome the cases. By the time this practice is read about, it may have been stopped. But if such practices are carried out, are you surprised that black immigrants are especially vulnerable to them? After all, they don't really count and they're a threat anyway. I wonder if Robert Mark included these shady lawyers amongst those he so roundly condemned?

5.
Fighting back

Musstaq Hussain works for a Nottingham textile firm, E.E. Jaffe. In May and June 1973 there was a strike over the dismissal of a worker, which was the culmination of a ten-month struggle to unionise. The workers wanted an increase on the £17.60 they were getting for a 40-hour week, proper lunch and tea breaks, canteen and toilet facilities. Musstaq Hussain:

> When I was eighteen I went to work for Jaffe's and then I went to Harwood Cash for a year and a half. There they made us work 60 hours a week, and we got the same basic as the whites got for 40 hours. At that time, I didn't have the courage to stand up against the employer because they used to say: 'If you don't like it, you can take your cards and go.' So most of us drifted away. I went back to Jaffe's for a year and then I went to Pakistan for six months.

On returning to England in 1972, Musstaq Hussain went back to Jaffe's. He says:

> All the workers were Pakistani at first, they thought of him not as an employer but as someone big who could do a lot of things to people. Everyone was divided up in that factory, one would be getting 30p and another 35p per hour. He said he was doing us a favour letting us work there, and later on we realised he wasn't doing us any favours, he should have been paying us the same as any English workers.

Encouraged by experience in another factory, the Pakistanis at Jaffe's organised a union and Musstaq Hussain was elected shop steward, whereupon the boss offered to make him a foreman if he resigned as shop steward. The workers started negotiations, but outside officials took over:

> After ten months of negotiating, we never got anywhere, and during that time we had four different union officials negotiating with Mr Jaffe, so none of them knew our case. When the fourth one came, we didn't know whether he was working for us or the management – he even left us standing in the rain while he sat in the office discussing the victimisation of Mr Sarhwu. That incident was the final straw and we came out on a four-week strike. But the union never did anything to help us.

The workers gradually drifted away to other jobs during the strike. Musstaq still believes that workers should unionise if they are not to be treated as cheap labour and he is encouraging his present workmates to join the union.

The practices that Musstaq has described are also used against British workers in the same situation, including paying different rates for the same job, and the offer of promotion to possible militants. Like many British workers, too, Musstaq Hussain came to learn the importance of unionisation. But this does not mean that the black workers' situation is exactly the same as that of the white worker. Black workers bear the unmistakeable mark of their colour; they are 'black workers' just as a woman is unmistakeably a 'woman worker' – and this has consequences for how other workers and trade unions see them. In this case, for example, it seems to have resulted in white workers turning a blind eye to black workers being used as cheap labour.

In fact, many black workers do badly-paid menial jobs. The expanding 'service' sector upon which 'affluence' depends is increasingly drawing in migrant workers to do what has traditionally been women's work. Thus until the Transport and General Workers' Union intervened, 400 Turkish workers in Wimpy Bars, Aberdeen Steak Houses and Texas Pancake Houses were earning such low wages that for a 90-hour week a Wimpy chef was getting £36.

But even when black workers have higher-status jobs,

like hospital doctors, they remain in lower positions. Thus black doctors are mainly *junior* hospital doctors; black nurses are State Enrolled Nurses, not State Registered Nurses. Similarly on the foundry floor and in the textile industry black workers have less skilled jobs or jobs in which they have to work harder or longer than their white workmates in order to earn the same money.

In Musstaq Hussain's industry, textiles, the most famous struggle involving coloured workers and trade unions is the Mansfield Hosiery case. Mansfield Hosiery makes pullovers. The process involves three groups of workers earning different wages: firstly, the knitters, who finish the work and receive about £45 a week; in 1972 there were eighty knitters, all white. The knitters are assisted by runners-on, who earn between £35 and £45 a week; three were white and eighty Asians. The lowest-paid job at about £23 a week, was bar-loading; all the bar-loaders were Asians.

In June 1972 the bar-loaders asked for a pay increase of £5 a week. The company said they would give this in return for increased productivity. In an industry marked by ruthless competition, closures and take-overs, 'increased productivity' normally means redundancies, with the remaining workers doing the extra work. The bar-loaders went on strike on 3 October, against union advice. All the other workers came out with them, although the knitters went back within a week. What underlay the strike action was the frustration felt by the bar-loaders, who were being kept from the better-paid knitters' jobs. The management agreed to train two Asian knitters, and on 10 October the white knitters struck in protest. This strike had been promised by the local union leadership if the whites were, in his words, 'flushed out' of the knitting jobs.

The company entered into a training agreement with the union (which was never signed) and offered the bar-loaders an extra £1 a week. The bar-loaders rejected this and with Asian workers at another company factory, making 400 in all, they struck on 27 October. The company dismissed them.

At the beginning of November the company recruited 41 white trainee knitters; but on the 16th at the union's request it stopped recruiting and withdrew notice to the strikers. The strikers returned the next day but they found the 41 new trainees still at work, so they struck again. The strike was made official on 4 December – after the strikers had occupied the union offices. The limited extent of the union's support is shown by their decision not to call out white workers, but only those involved in the grievance.

The Department of Employment then conducted an enquiry into the situation. The report criticised management and unions and said the Asians were misguided in not going through proper channels with their grievances. It also recommended establishing a pool of vacancies for the 41 knitters. The Asians said they would return to work if guaranteed 30 of these places – but they finally returned to work when it was agreed that a Department of Employment official would sit on the selection panel.

The atmosphere on the return to work was described by the union as 'strained', and there were allegations that white knitters were refusing to train Asian trainees. A knitters' leader then pointed out that if the conflict went on, the management would close the mill and they would all be out of a job. In the end 28 Asians were selected for training as knitters, rejecting efforts by the white workers to persuade them to give up eight posts.

In this series of events white workers supported black workers in their demand for money but opposed them on questions of promotion. The white unionists wanted to keep the best jobs for themselves and felt especially vulnerable given the very uncertain state of the industry. It was easy in a situation where the government and the public defined the black population as a problem and a threat to see them also as the cause of the insecurity that threatened white workers. What persuaded them to return to work was, apparently, the threat of complete closure; it was more important to keep working than to protect job 'rights' and the cosy arrangement between union and management that ensured those rights.

The situation was typical of the small manufacturing unit caught in a highly competitive market between rising costs and monopoly buyers who are able to force prices down. The easiest cost for the firm to cut is the cost of wages; one way to keep wages down is to hire labour of a kind that the unions will not be anxious to defend – black labour. The use of cheap labour keeps *all* wages down, so together black and white workers could have forced all their wages up. But it was easy for management to divide the workers because the whites feared loss of privileges. However poorly paid they were, the white workers could feel superior to the Asian workers – and in many such situations (though not this one) this is about *all* they can hope to gain. A weak union with a history of collaboration with management ensured that the Mansfield system of industrial relations was not questioned or its implications exposed.

In May 1974 there began a strike at Imperial Typewriters, Leicester, which lasted for three months. It was the subject of numerous enquiries and reports. The background was simple: exploited workers fighting a company *and* a racist union. The Imperial Typewriter Company was well suited to benefit from the arrival of East African Asians in Leicester, and by May 1974 1,100 out of 1,600 of the workers were Asians. The work involved assembling the parts of typewriters made in Germany, Holland and Japan. The basic rate of pay was £18 for women and £25 for men, with bonuses for the production of 200 machines a day.

An Asian woman describes her working day:

> I have to be at work at 9 and before that – at ten to nine –
> I take my son to school. I have to wake up at 6 o'clock
> every morning. I get all my children dressed and give
> them breakfast. Then I make my husband some tea. By
> then it's nearly 8 o'clock. Then my husband goes to work.
> He has to be there at 8. After that sometimes I have to
> help my children with their homework – reading, spell-
> ing, things like that. Then at about 8.30 my 8-year-old

daughters leave together for school. They go on their own. Then I have to put my two other children – one is 5½ and the other is 4 – in the nursery. After that I rush straight to work.

I work until 3 and my husband works until 5. At 3 I go straight from the factory to get my two children from the nursery. And soon after I get home my other two children also come back from school. That's about 4 o'clock. I give them some milk and a wash and then start cooking because my husband eats every day at 6. So by 6 I must have the food ready. I like to put my children to bed early. So after cooking I give them something to eat. I like them to go to bed by 6.30, but sometimes it gets a little later. After that there are always clothes to wash and also the dishes. I like to finish all the work just before I sit down. We usually listen to the news at 9 o'clock on the radio before going to sleep.

On 1 May, 27 women and 12 men – all of section 61 – came out on strike. The production line had been speeded. In discussion with the factory convenor (T&GWU) they discovered that under a 1972 agreement, their bonus should have been paid for 168 machines completed. This meant £4 a week to the workers. So they added to their demands for a new wage agreement the payment of the bonus backdated to January 1973.

The strikers were also concerned about the quality of the trade union officials. There was only one Asian on the shop stewards' committee, and section 61 demanded the right to elect their own shop steward. The Asians thought that the stewards were almost part of management; for example:

I went to our shop steward one day and explained that the 22 target was too high. I also told her that the supervisor had asked us to oil our own machines that morning. Normally the machines are oiled before we come in. I told her that oiling was not our job and that management was always trying to make us do more work for the same pay. She told me not to make a fuss over such a small thing. That's the kind of shop steward she is.

In addition they demanded an end to petty restrictions on washing time, tea and lunch breaks and toilet breaks which were not imposed upon white workers. 'Race relations' in the firm were not good; it seemed as if the white workers behaved as if the black workers did not exist.

> The other thing is that every morning when we come to work at 8 o'clock we have to stand in a long queue to clock in. I try and come at five to eight because we are paid according to time. Many of us have noticed that the white women push past us and clock in first. The foreman at the gate never tells them to stand in the queue. None of us would dare to do that. Why should they be allowed to do it – not once or twice but every day?

> The setters (we have all white setters) set the white women's machines first and take more trouble over them. Ours they do last and they don't even do them properly. So we have to work slower and then, with piece work, we earn less money. Before our machines are set we have to wait. So we asked for waiting time but they wouldn't give that to us. White women also get jobs of their choice – they can choose their jobs. But we have to do what the setter gives us to do.

By 7 May, 500 workers were out and the production of the factory was down to 50 per cent. The local trade union convenor and the Labour MP both tried to persuade the workers to go back to work. The quickest way to resolve the strike would have been for all the workers to have come out in support of the original strikers. The management would have been beaten quickly and the strike finished on the workers' terms. But that didn't happen.

On the 10th the company sacked 75 of the original strikers. Section 61 had thrown up two leaders, Hasmukh Khetani and N.C.Patel, who were only 21 years old and quite free from the red-tape tradition of trade union organisation. The T&GWU negotiator then discovered an old rule that said shop stewards could only be elected after two years at the factory; that cut out Khetani and Patel. The T&GWU local convenor said he would talk to any strikers except these two. The union never made the strike official, and this was itself the subject of severe criticism by the strikers and eventually the object of a special enquiry by the T&GWU at regional level.

Many young people were involved in the strike and it was a source of some alarm to some sections of the white population that long-haired, brightly-dressed Asian youths were appearing on the scene. It is West Indian youths who are meant to be 'disaffected' and troublesome; Asians are meant to be quiet, obedient and hard-working.

The strikers were never anti-union; they stressed that the speed of the production line was of interest to every worker in the factory. What the strikers wanted was a *better* union, more responsive to the needs of the workers. They then went on to demonstrate what more responsive unionism was like.

Their picketing was not half-hearted; anything from 50 to 200 workers were out on the picket-line, making a solid show of strength and determination to management and blacklegs alike. Instead of working through committees and behind-the-scenes negotiations the strike was controlled by a daily mass grievance meeting. It was described by a reporter as having evolved from 'a single forum for a catalogue of ills to a living instrument of the mass of workers'. The report added: 'Here there can be no separation of "leaders" from "led" . . . Every decision of the strike committee, every move and ploy by management, each newspaper report and meeting addressed is communicated within the mass meeting.' At the beginning these meetings were tape-recorded so that the committee could be sure to miss nothing and would be able to put every grievance into the form of a proposal.

It is not surprising that in the strike the women emerged as a very powerful and a very militant force. As housewives and mothers they were acutely aware of the meaning of low wages and rising prices. Instead of just supporting the men, the women made equal pay a priority in the demands of the strikers.

Imperial Typewriters is one of a whole class of firms

likely to use female labour in order to assemble goods cheaply near the main market. These industries have parts made overseas and then assembled by the cheapest possible labour near the point of sale. Assembly work is typically 'women's work'. Very great efforts have been made throughout Europe to get more women into the labour force, especially in light industry and services. Those who, in the UK, call for lowering the school-leaving age to 14 on proof of literacy may have young people in mind as a further source of labour. But if women, blacks and young people are sources of relatively cheap labour, how much more exploited will be labour that is female *and* black, or young *and* black?

The strikers at Imperial discovered that they had power, that they could mobilise and organise, that they could run their own affairs and meet the challenge of multinational corporations. Mass pickets and strike meetings were broken up by the police, men were charged with offences arising from picketing; from this the strikers learnt how to organise themselves for defence in the courts and were able to demonstrate against the prosecution. Their strength reached right down into the community; the women were part of the strike, some Asian landlords were willing to wait for their rent, shopkeepers were willing to give credit or put a little extra in the shopping bag. This is not, of course, to paint a sentimental picture of complete harmony and solidarity – many Asians went on working, and many landlords would not wait for the rent. Crucially, the union did not encourage white workers to unite with the blacks in their fight against the bosses.

Money – although not enough to meet the strikers' needs – came in from further afield: Birmingham Sikh Temple, Southall Indian Workers' Association, Birmingham Anti-Racist Committee, European Workers' Action Committee, a women's conference in Edinburgh. Local factories with Asian workers supported the pickets and two factories collected more than £300. To keep the strikers together over the works holiday period, coach trips and concerts were arranged. Community solidarity and *racial* solidarity were very important, however. The four local factories with T&GWU branches with high Asian membership promised a 24-hour stoppage whenever it was needed. This kind of solidarity was the *only* basis the strikers had to organise on. What they mainly lacked was industrial solidarity at their place of work. They all lived locally and were a community, their grievances had a substantial racial element, the union offered no support; so they started from there and worked with what they had. If they were surprised with what they achieved, they had no need to be; they used the power that is there when men and women act together. In the end there were pickets on the shops and offices of Imperial or Litton (the parent company) in London, Leeds, Birmingham, Nottingham, Liverpool, Newcastle, Sheffield and Hull. In many cases the pickets were organised by young blacks, but they were often joined by white workers.

With the relatively open structure of the strikers' organisation they were able to go a step beyond the fight for their immediate goals in the factory and in the community. They were able – from personal experience now – to discuss the role of the police and the courts, and the activities of the National Front (very much in evidence); and in the circumstances how could they not discuss the role of Asian women, now standing shoulder to shoulder with the men, and the problems of African politics which had catapulted them into Leicester? The Imperial strikers were showing what organised workers could do, and what their power could achieve. They held up a mirror to British trade unionists and invited them to learn from what they saw. The impetus of Asian militancy could have revived and revitalised the trade union movement for all employed at Imperial and in the locality. But prejudice or fear of management prevented this.

The end of the strike was not very spectacular and no major victories were won. The strikers got their jobs back, with no victimisation of strike leaders; negotiations were to be conducted with the company over wages and with the union over the election of shop stewards. The return to work was to be phased over two weeks to avoid antagonising the blacklegs. Half the Asian work force remained at work throughout the strike and only one white woman joined the strikers. To this extent the strike was a failure.

The strikers' 'community' was important in the Imperial Typewriter dispute, the community consisting not of fellow trade unionists but of members of the local Asian society, the wives and families of the strikers and Asian members of the main trade union. The whole community learnt also that they needed industrial organisation if they wanted to consolidate their community power. Community power alone is not enough to achieve significant political changes. But the effects of the strike, which was not a startling success *as a strike*, were even more widespread.

Kenilworth Components made plastic fittings mainly for the fashion shoe trade. The twenty men in the factory had to work a 60-hour week in five twelve-hour shifts, for which they were paid a little over £30. There were also 30 women workers in the factory who were working a 42-hour week for £12 (the company said £15). This wage was for very unskilled work, but the wages were not adequate for any job.

The women realised that they were being underpaid; most of them spoke little or no English at all, but they had been in Leicester long enough to know that it was an affluent city in which £12 was an inadequate weekly wage. Some of the women were the breadwinners in families in which the men had been unable to get jobs, so they felt the pinch especially sharply. They did not really know what to do, so they held a meeting outside the factory to discuss their situation. This meeting was seen by a T&GWU branch secretary from a nearby factory; he was himself an Asian and he went over to offer his help and sign them up. The T&GWU made the strike official but never paid the strikers any strike pay.

It is hard for the average English person to understand the full significance of what was happening. It is 'common knowledge' that Asian women are shy and subservient to their menfolk, docile and obedient in all things. This may be a caricature, but it is a fact that Asian women are not known for being outspoken in public. The women at Kenilworth were angry and they were on strike; they chose as their spokeswomen the only people they could choose – the two girls who spoke good English – and these were two of the youngest, Bhanti Rajami (16) and Vilash Balhia (19).

The union negotiated a quick return to work, but when the women turned up the management told them that eleven would have to leave because of a fall in demand for plastic mouldings. Not surprisingly Bhanti Rajami and Vilash Balhia were on the list of eleven. Old-timers at Kenilworth said that the management had been known to sack the whole work force for joining a union. The one man who joined the strike had previously been threatened with the sack for joining a union. The women refused to return to work on those terms, and the local manager threatened to close the factory (a threat later repudiated by the parent company).

At this stage the Imperial Typewriter strike became important. It was obvious that the Asians were in a militant mood and that they felt the Imperial strike to have been a victory. There would clearly have been mass support from the Asian community for the women at Kenilworth. A joint meeting was held between the Kenilworth strikers and the Imperial strike committee. But the government and unions were afraid that the racial bitterness created by the Imperial strike would spill over and inflame the Kenilworth dispute and perhaps the whole of Leicester. With government intervention the strike was brought to an end. The authorities were so afraid of racial conflict that they asked Kenilworth not to respond in a tough way to the industrial dispute. This somewhat silenced the management, who later claimed that because of this enforced silence they were misrepresented throughout the affair. The women are now working a 30-hour week at 45p an hour; this is a considerable improvement on the 28–30p an hour they were getting before. This still only gives a wage of £13.50, but the women can claim unemployment benefit for two days of the week.

The financial settlement is not the most important result of the strike. The real significance was noted by a business correspondent in the *Sunday Times* who said that, for the women: 'Standing up for themselves has proved worthwhile. And for a lot of people in Leicester it has proved a salutary reminder that the inarticulate, too, need – and can win – effective protection.' That protection comes from acting together with the support of others, whether the 'others' be the wider membership of a union, or, in this case, the Asian community.

Mansfield Hosiery and Kenilworth Plastics were both small companies tied either by markets or mergers to much bigger companies. A high rate of production and low costs were essential to both of them. In the one case they had 'sweetheart' agreements with the union which kept the blacks in low-wage jobs; in the other they were simply anti-union. Imperial is part of the gigantic empire of Litton Industries Ltd, which has 1,660 subsidiaries. It is using cheap labour in foreign countries to make the parts and then the cheapest possible labour near the European market to assemble them.

In a big industrial manufacturing corporation the management's greatest need is for a large work force that will work continuously and consistently. Wage cutting may be important but the possession of a stable work force is very much more important. If reduction in labour costs were the only consideration then a big international corporation might just as well move all its operations overseas. Henry Ford hired a private army to deal with his workers, but today companies can get a state to do the job for them – thus BLMC employs 3800 workers in South Africa.

The Ford Motor Company is one which has specialised in the use of black migrant and captive labour. In its earliest days in Detroit, Ford used immigrant workers from the

American South. Today in the Philippines it pays skilled workers an average of 30c an hour, which is considerably less than the $7.50 per hour paid to Ford workers in the United States. Ford at Dagenham suffers from very high labour turn-over; it offers such poor working conditions that fewer English workers are now being recruited, and to maintain any labour force at all the company has to rely more heavily on West Indian, Asian and Irish workers.

Workers are recruited on the basis of advertisements promising £47 a week. When the workers have settled in they are moved to sections doing permanent day work without over-time; for some this means a wage cut of around £15. One permanent feature of the work is lay-offs; this is a characteristic of the motor industry, which experiences fluctuations in the markets for its product and fluctuations in supplies from the small firms that produce the parts and materials needed in making a car. The work situation is, in a word, unstable.

The brunt of 'managing' this work force falls upon the foremen. 'At Ford's the foremen think they are God Al-mighty,' said a worker. Many foremen are ex-shop stewards, men who prefer individual advancement to collective security. But the conflict and tension of supervision have led to ill-health among the foremen and occasional outbreaks of violence against them. As over 60 per cent of the assembly line workers are black, Ford needs to ensure that it has black foremen. 'They no doubt need black foremen to control the situation as much as the Commissioner of Police needs black policemen,' was how one commentator put it. For this reason there is no racial discrimination in promotion. This is a very clear case where non-discrimination is in management's interest. The enquirer who asks, 'Why is Ford so keen to eliminate discrimination?' will soon find himself up against questions about Ford and Ford management that are of vital interest to *all* workers.

Ford maintains industrial order by keeping the men moving from job to job, and especially moving the militants and keeping pressure on anyone who looks like making trouble.

The task is made easier by the very high labour turnover which means that dissatisfied workers just drop out. In this situation the Asian workers can feel especially weak and unable to fight back. One worker reported:

> I went to see a friend. He was sitting, crying, at home with his wife and kids. He didn't know whom to turn to. He said, 'God knows what I'm doing. I'm so terrified by the foreman. They push you all the time, even push you by hand, to make you work. I don't know what to do. I can't carry on like this.' He wanted badly to leave Ford's, but he had only just arrived in London, and he didn't know to whom to turn for work.

In such conditions the management is able to find men willing to inform on others in return for favours, the workers are divided by language and race. There is no unity, no common sense of grievance among them. It is easy to impose lay-offs as a way of cutting wages and easy to keep pressure on through foremen.

The foremen have been, perhaps, the weakest link in the chain of control, and more recently the men have been fighting back; 'once you can get the foremen off your back you can begin to get some freedom'. So far sanctions against the foremen have been confined to name-calling and jeering, but just doing this gave the men sufficient unity and sense of freedom to mount a small stoppage on the assembly line in protest against failure to pay lay-off pay. In September 1974 the foremen struck because of their fear of physical assault, and the workers themselves then continued to keep production going at Dagenham through their own version of 'workers' control'. This has only been possible because the workers have been able to 'unite and fight' rather than dividing against themselves on racial lines. As has so often been the case in the history of the working class, it has been management that has played a very important role in driving workers into militant solidarity and showing them that strength lies only in unity. Ford is a very small beginning in which the struggle for autonomy at work is as important as the struggle for wages. But it is a beginning nonetheless.

Away from the heat and noise of the motor car production line, in the 'cool and calm' of the hospital, black workers have recently been active in strikes of nurses, technicians and radiographers. Anyone watching television news broadcasts of the nurses' strike could not fail to notice the high proportion of coloured faces amongst those walking from the wards to the picket-line or mass meeting.

A nurse says:

> I came to this country in 1962 when I was 17. I went to look for a job and the Youth Employment Service suggested that I go for a job in a factory. I didn't want to work in a factory – but I didn't know what I wanted to do – I didn't really want to do nursing as such. I went to a London teaching hospital to train as a nurse. They said I would have to work as an auxilliary first because of my age. I now know this isn't true.

What this girl did was menial work on the wards. But: 'to me it has always just been a job. I trained because I couldn't see what else there was; now it is a way of earning a living.'

As a way of earning a living nursing is similar to other service industries in two ways: it is largely staffed by women and it is an occupation in which the employer has consistently refused to pay adequate wages. Instead, workers are recruited from overseas. In 1970 about 19,000 student nurses were admitted to Britain. Nurses come from Ireland, the West Indies, and increasingly from Malaysia, Mauritius and Hong Kong. This is also true of other European countries; one German regional director of a health scheme has commented that he 'cleaned out the Philippines' and was now recruiting in South Korea.

Many of these overseas students are directed to the SEN courses (State Enrolled Nurse) rather than the SRN (State Registered Nurse). This is often presented as a choice between the two- and three-year course but in reality it is a choice between joining the professional (SRN) nursing service, with prospects for promotion, or remaining in a semi- or non-professional role with no promotion prospects and lower pay. In mid-1974 SRN pay went from £1,338 to £1,725; if they get to the 'top' they can achieve £3,810 – not generous salaries by any means. SEN salaries went from £1,200 to £1,755. An unqualified nursing auxiliary can earn from £816 (at 18) to £1,293.

These grades represent a strict hierarchy of professional status and power of control over others. 'I find nurses are very conscious of what positions they hold – even some of the black ones,' said a black SEN. 'All of us have to do a lot of things they (nurses) do, except we don't give injections or write reports. We have to admit the patients, we have to make beds, take them to . . . treatment, we do everything they do . . . only they sit in the office. We are the ones outside with the patients all the time.'

The overseas student nurses are in a very poor position; they do much of the menial work, but how can they complain when their work permits have to be renewed every six months through the hospital? Their position is much closer to that of all Commonwealth workers under the 1971 Act. The insult added to the rigours of hospital and ward hierarchy is that of racial discrimination – it is not uncommon for doctors, including black doctors, to ask a black nurse (SRN) to 'get me a nurse'. 'Doctors treat you terrible and the black ones are just as bad. They just completely ignore black nurses once there's a white nurse there.'

One response to the exploitation of nurses was the strike; another has been the rise of agency nursing. By working for an agency a nurse is much more free to arrange her working hours to suit her family; it can enable her to do two jobs, in fact.

> I work night shifts. You may get £2 or £3 more than on days, but for me it's much more convenient because . . . it fits in with my housework. Most of the night staff are black. Night nurses are black because they have children

and it's more convenient for them to be at home in the days to see after the children. If you work days you're not in to send them off to school, you're not there to receive them when they come back, and you have to get somebody to look after them. With nights, you can actually put them off to bed before going to work.

This manner of working can involve appalling exploitation of black female labour; but it brings some flexibility to an exploited way of life and frees the woman from the rigid hierarchy of the hospital. In London, where there are about 2,700 agency nurses, some hospitals have more agency nurses than any others on the night shift. This is a sobering thought for any potential patient, that his or her care may depend on a woman who has just completed a hard day's work.

It is not only black women who work for agencies: 'There are nurses from all over the world working for agencies. I feel very sorry for the girls, say, from the Philippines and Malaysia who don't speak English very well and who are being exploited. They remind me of when I first started training,' says an agency nurse from Barbados.

During the 1974 strike, the Confederation of Health Service Employees (COHSE) decided not to work with agency nurses, for several reasons. At the simplest level, agency nurses can be seen as scab labour, willing to take on jobs at poor wages and not joining the fight of the majority of nurses against bad pay. As long as there are agency nurses, the hospitals will not be forced into paying adequate wages to the 'career' nurse. No doubt an element of racial hostility also entered into the support given to the ban by some white nurses.

Agency nurses have also come to symbolise the neglect of the health service and the failure of successive governments to pay the respect due to some of the most socially useful workers in Britain. NHS nurses have reason to be wary of agency nurses, who are less tied down to the hospital hierarchy than the 'professionals'.

But it is *both* the inadequacy of wages *and* the structure of hospital employment (rigid hours and rigid hierarchies) that have created the demand and personnel for agencies. COHSE has campaigned for better wages so successfully that in September 1974 nurses were given a backdated pay rise of up to 58 per cent at the lower levels; but it left the question of control and hierarchy untouched. From this point of view nurses who prefer agency work might argue that COHSE keep the issue to a narrowly economic one and avoid the key issues of status and control and the employment conditions of married women. COHSE would thus have had a politically conservative role.

In fact, the conflict between COHSE and agency nurses cuts right across race and rank and goes to the heart of the NHS – the health industry. It raises the basic questions about why we seem able to make health provision only on the basis of exploited labour – especially exploited female labour.

Officially most trade unions are against racial discrimination, and their conferences have resolutions (usually not debated) to that effect, accompanied by much rhetoric about the brotherhood of man and the common struggle of all workers. Their conferences are also usually full of socialist rhetoric; the trade union bureaucrats have been as successful in bringing about racial equality as they have in bringing in socialism. 'Policy' usually consists of doing nothing because to do anything is to draw attention to race, or to make the situation worse, or to create a privileged group of black workers. The keynote is found in Tom Jackson's bland assertion that 'Everyone in our union gets the same service'. What this attitude fails to take into account is that while black workers are workers, like their mates, they also have special work problems *because they are black*, and for no other reason.

What the national 'leaders' of the trade unions have done does not impinge in any significant way on the daily life of any workers, and certainly not black workers. There can be various responses to the work situation: workers dropping out from Ford, finding alternative employers in nursing, organising within the local union structure at Kenilworth and organising against it at Imperial and Mansfield Hosiery. Some black and white workers are hostile to unions, and white workers can be hostile or friendly to black workers.

The record of some trade unions falls far short of what is needed to cope with the problem of racism in Britain. The T&GWU has a good record of statements against racism and an appalling record of racialist behaviour. We have already seen that the Kenilworth strikers received no strike pay. In addition the union's report on the Imperial dispute completely vindicated the strikers by pointing out that the local union leadership was flouting the national agreement on bonuses and that there was little opportunity for rank and file grievances to emerge through rank and file leadership. It looks as if the local leadership was trying to turn a challenge to their power into a racial dispute; mobilising whites against blacks. There was and is a very real danger that such attempts will succeed and when black workers form their own unions the management will then be able to play union against union. The union's national leadership has taken no effective action against this kind of activity by local officials. But they would not need to do so if the rank and file were willing to put their own local branches in order. Racialism weakens unions and it weakens them where it hurts most, in their conflicts with management for wages, better conditions and a measure of control over the work situation.

At the purely economic level, black workers, like white workers, are 'hands' to be hired or fired by management; they are there to work for others. Their problems at work are the problems of every other worker: wages, overtime, the control of the work situation, speed-ups of the assembly line, trade union recognition and so on. But 'work' means different things to different groups of workers: some men and women have training, skills or positions which give them a lot of control over their own work and how they organise their working day, and if they occupy management positions they have control over other men and women as well. Nine million workers are in trade unions; they tend to be in more stable jobs with a degree of job security and wages protected by the union. There are workers in small factories and workshops, restaurants, hotels and other service industries, including the public sector, who are seldom unionised; they usually have poorer wages than workers in unions. Then there are workers, usually without special skills, who move from job to job, perhaps with spells of unemployment, who may belong to a number of unions or none. Finally there are women who do a full day's work as mothers and housewives and then take part-time or evening jobs, usually for very poor wages. Black workers are to be found concentrated in some kinds of jobs and hardly at all in others. Each of these situations creates somewhat different roles and problems for the black worker and calls forth different reactions from black workers, and from white workers in response to their reactions.

One reaction is that of many West Indians or youths of West Indian descent, who have seen the menial work that their parents have done and have foreseen the menial jobs that are awaiting them at the end of an inadequate education. They are dropping out of the labour market and refusing to work altogether. These groups of young people are increasingly involved in hostilities and violence with the police; part of the police's job is to get them off the streets, and that means back to work. They have also been the subject of some rather anxious reports. No doubt the unemployed and disaffected black youth will be the first candidates for compulsory deportation, if that comes about, 'for their own good' and for the good of those who have 'settled down here' in low-paid menial jobs.

One case study that has not been written is that of black workers breaking a white workers' strike. It has not been written simply because no such case is known to exist.

On the other hand, the Indian Workers Association has unionised non-union men and then 'delivered' whole new branches to the union. Black workers have shown unshakeable solidarity in London bus strikes and have been generous in their support of workers in other firms, irrespective of their colour. The Fine Tubes factory in Plymouth was in dispute for three years, and the men tried to raise nationwide support. One of the workers addressed a supporting meeting in Loughborough:

> 'During our strike we needed the support of other workers to boycott supplies to Fine Tubes. We went to the union of one of the factory's main suppliers and the officials indecisively told us that they didn't know if the workers would support us. Because of our experience we talked to the workers directly. When we went to the meeting we were surprised to find that it was mainly black workers who pledged their support. And throughout our battle with Fine Tubes, no supplies have come through those workers.'

There have, however, been cases of white workers crossing black workers' picket lines – sometimes egged on by the National Front. Union officials who negotiated the return to work at Imperial also addressed the (mainly white) meeting held to protest at the settlement terms, and they adopted anti-Asian positions. Perhaps given the general racial climate I have described, the lack of rank-and-file racism is a tribute to the average worker, who has not been well served by his union leaders. When black and white workers are actually brought into conflict by market forces or scheming management, it is not at all remarkable that men should fly to the defence of their immediate economic interests, as at Mansfield Hosiery. In times of economic uncertainty and inflation it is too easy to tell workers to look beyond today and 'wider' influences at work in society. They are concerned with the next meal.

It is a fact that West Indian workers get only 75 per cent of the average white wage, and the Asian worker 80 to 85 per cent. The reason for this difference is not hard to see, given the concentration of West Indians in the service sector of the economy.

But against this, the most exploited workers have come

to realise their plight. They have found that they do not have to rely upon union officials to save them; they can do it themselves. When they do they are very powerful. And when they can call on worker solidarity across race lines they are even more powerful. They have learned that even if you are an Asian woman who does not speak English, you can resist the boss. If you are 16 or 21, a boy or a girl, you can serve your workmates in an active capacity. If you are black, you can still find some white support. What is more, the cases we have described show the great strength and imagination, and, at times, youthful energy, that lies in the whole black community – not just on the shop floor – and how this can and must be motivated to support the struggle of workers. This is far more important than Head Office in London giving you its blessing.

But, as the discussion of Imperial typewriters showed, resistance does not stop at the factory gates. Blacks are responding in a variey of ways outside their places of work.

Some responses are of a negative kind and may prove to be counter-productive. For example, when black youths drop out of the labour market they isolate themselves from industrial exploitation. They declare themselves unwilling to take the menial jobs that their parents accepted, but they also run the risk of becoming involved in petty, semi-criminal activities that can be of no advantage to themselves or anyone else. Black youth already attract discriminatory and violent behaviour from the police, and the drop-out response amplifies this behaviour. It might, as was suggested earlier, lead to demands for deportation.

Nonetheless there are lessons to be learnt even from the responses of the police and the courts. In 1973 a youth was stabbed while in a queue at a fish and chip shop in South London. The police arrived and a crowd gathered. The police began to panic and tried to push the crowd back, but the crowd was under pressure from people pouring out of a fair in Brockwell Park. The police drew their truncheons and laid into the crowd. A general fight developed, a policeman was hurt and reinforcements sent for. A police riot ensued; they attacked people all around them and lost control of themselves. Three black youths were arrested, one to the accompaniment of the following exchange between policemen: 'That's one of them'; 'No it isn't, but he'll do.' Another youth was already known to the police and an easy target for arrest.

The youths finally appeared at the Old Bailey. They had some difficulty in getting witnesses to come forward, perhaps partly reflecting the lack of vigour shown by the defending lawyers, who certainly made no effort to bring out the full significance of police behaviour. The three youths were convicted and each given three years in prison. One later won an appeal against conviction, but the other two were not so fortunate. Three of the constables involved were given awards for bravery.

After this the stunned black community in Brixton began to mobilise. On 20 March a meeting was held in Brixton town hall at which a fund was started for the three and a committee formed to campaign for them. On the 27th the Tulse Hill Students' Collective organised a meeting attended by 70 children from nine to 17 years old. The collective which had raised £100, urged other schools to raise money. At the meeting a Black Students' Action Committee was formed. On 30 March, a 500-strong demonstration and a public meeting took place to spread information about the case. Then on 3 April 1,000 school pupils, most of them black, came out on strike. They held a rally and march – parading past the local court, the police station, Tulse Hill School, where another 100 pupils joined them, and Brockwell Park.

This represents a very considerable mobilisation of black youth. While their main aim is to free the three boys, they are discovering more about the police and the courts; they are having to ask questions about school and work. Above all, they are discovering the strength of their own community, the strength of youth organised. Anger, morale and strength are all raised by joint activity. What the outcome of this mobilisation is to be we can not know, but for many black youths who are already mobilised and for those who are yet to be reached by it the mobilisation could mark a turning point in their political consciousness and careers – whatever forms these may take.

For a city with such a long history of black settlement, the city of Liverpool still has remarkably few blacks in public employment, and discrimination in housing has led to concentration of the black population. One community action project, the Liverpool 8 Black Community Action Group, is attempting to mobilise youth in a way that constrasts sharply with the developments after Brockwell Park:

> The education system seemed geared to destroying our black identity in school . . . this then leaves us at an early and impressionable age in a state of absolute nakedness as regards any real identity. All we are left with is confusion, frustration, and a deep stirring urge to lash out, hit back or go searching for what we believe to be our true identity. This is why we attach so much importance to our black studies and our free black history and culture library, as they are a basic need of Liverpool-born black people who are in search of that identity.

The Action Group has a black studies programme that enables young people to discover who they are and to find out what kind of a world they live in. What is particularly interesting in cases like these is that because of very obvious colour differences it has been easier for black children to react against the *white* middle-class values of the education system (which stress achievement and success to young blacks, to whom these are denied) than it has for working-class children to question the *middle-class* values of the schools. The working-class response has really been one of *accepting* educational values as given and therefore, to some extent, middle-class images of working-class people. Perhaps one result of the demand for black studies will be a long overdue demand for working-class studies in our schools.

The Action Group also runs workshops, especially for those recently out of school. 'We hope to be able to show our young workers different ways they can apply themselves more fully and effectively; such as through the pottery course we aim to introduce them to art as a source of income and career . . . The money that each member of group makes will be divided.' Such groups do not run without support, and in order to sustain their highly constructive work they have to rely upon other organisations and individuals. Hopefully such supporters will be drawn into asking some of the same questions that are posed by the young people of Liverpool 8.

The Institute of Race Relations in London was founded in 1956 as a learned organisation 'to encourage and facilitate the study of the relations between the races everywhere'. It was a non-political organisation that made no official statements on any topic but which felt itself obliged to inform those responsible for making decisions in the field of race relations. Some very good studies were conducted, which formed the basis of serious thought and study of 'race relations'. The Institute's council was made up of senior members of the academic establishment, politicians and businessmen. The Institute received grants from a number of big businesses and from foundations such as the Ford Foundation. It also held some rather exclusive conferences for businessmen and politicians; one in November 1962 looked at the problems of the independence of post-Imperial countries. But *whose* problems were they? The last discussion in the conference was on 'problems of the banks, the extractive industries and the diplomats'. They were Britain's banks, industries and diplomats. The discussion was about the possibilities of maximising profits from newly independent countries.

With the rise of racism in Britain the Institute continued to address Top People, without any noticeable effect; it did not address itself to the black people who were the objects of so many of its studies. Gradually the people working for the Institute came to ask questions about this; and then one young scholar wrote a paper investigating the connections between Council members and racial exploitation overseas. The demands for his resignation precipitated the first of a series of crises within the Institute in which the people working for the organisation began to seek a greater say in the day-to-day conduct of its work. They also tried to use the research of the Institute in order to say something useful to the black population. This was defined as a breach of the Institute's 'non-political' status. It came to a head in March 1972 when the Council tried to close down the journal *Race Today* and sack the director of the Institute. There was a massive mobilisation of Institute members and the Council members suffered an overwhelming and humiliating defeat. The Establishment men on the Council resigned and went off to back new kinds of venture. They also took their money with them and persuaded their business friends to withdraw funds and other kinds of support from the Institute.

The Institute had been housed off Piccadilly; it employed many staff and was generally well-provided for. It now exists on a shoe-string, from day to day, understaffed in a basement. Its political wing has been hived off to avoid problems with the charity laws; as 'Towards Racial Justice', it publishes *Race Today*. But the Institute's library is now accessible to and used by black groups and has a section for black children. It was *Race Today* that instigated a national campaign in support of the Imperial typewriter strikers. So even in the 'academic' world the struggle for racial justice has been brought to earth, even against very tough odds. Many whites have received a political education in the Institute during its past ten years and have become politically radicalised.

The countryman, asked the way to Dublin, replied: 'If I was going to Dublin I wouldn't start from here.' In real life we all start from where we are, whatever theories others have about what we should do. Black citizens start from where they are: in the hosiery mills, on the assembly line, in the street, making pottery or writing poetry. Without picking on a series of success stories we have been able to see the tremendous strength that lies in the black community. One reason why the

Imperial strikers were so strong was that, like the miners, they were able to rely upon the support of a whole community. The new lesson in this was the revelation of the unity of the women's struggle with the men's. Men, women, blacks and whites may have some divergent interests, but they have certain common interests which demand that we face and overcome racism and sexism. 'People who had at the beginning been scared and shy had grown enormously in stature.'

Black militancy in any form now draws opposition. For example the National Front was encouraging white workers not to work alongside Imperial strikers, and a march it had planned for Manchester was shifted to Leicester in order to capitalise on the racial antagonism that had been aroused there. Strike leaders receive letters like: 'Get out of this country you curry-faced swine. This green and pleasant land of ours is no place for you or your caste. Remember the stoning of British soldiers at Calcutta. We shall have you watched and any more trouble – look out.'

There are conflicts within black communities, like any other, and these may be overcome for the duration of the particular dispute or campaign. This is to say that the black community is much like any other community. Constant economic and political pressure can not only lead to political solidarity, it can also lead to men and women falling out with one another. The black 'community' does not really exist as at Mansfield Hosiery or in Liverpool 8. There are communities of Muslims, Hindus, Punjabis, Bangladeshis, Barbadians and Jamaicans. Some East African Asians are small capitalists and some West Indians are crooks. One practice has not been eliminated. Because many Asians have no English or speak it very poorly, and because they need contacts in finding jobs, there has grown up a group of middlemen in the labour market. These middlemen usually have good English and are well established in a firm. They demand a fee for finding a job for a man, then a cut of his wages plus presents from time to time. If the worker is illegal or illicit immigrant he is especially vulnerable to this kind of treatment. Some white foremen also learn this practice and immigrants have to pay, say, £50 to get a job. 'They pay the money to foremen and supervisors at factories. These immigrants may have had difficulty getting work because of their lack of English or their lack of skill. Some agree to pay a weekly amount so they can get a job. I know of this happening in towns in Yorkshire and the Midlands.'

The potential for division and strife are there as in any society; but we have seen some of the ways in which this can be overcome. At the more overtly political level there are organisations growing amongst black workers; the various wings of the Indian Workers' Association have been established in Britain for some time. The Black Workers' Movement has the following strategy:

> 1. Mobilising the strength of the whole black class in the community and in the factory. 2. Seeking to talk to white workers and demanding they support our struggles (as we give ours) in their own class interest. But refusing to concede to racist hostility if they refuse. 3. Internationalising our struggle wherever possible.

The Black People's Freedom Movement asserts the need to fight racism as such, to forge links between black workers and to form black caucuses. The Black Workers' Co-ordinating Committee and the Black Unity and Freedom Party urge the 'importance of a trade union that truly represents the interests of workers' and the development of 'the working-class ideology of revolutionary and scientific socialism amongst all workers, especially Black workers.'

So the black response, halting and faulty at times, can be found in activities ranging from dropping out, through social work and community action, to industrial activity and trade unionsim, to revolutionary socialism. Debate, conflict over best policies and between groups is inevitable and healthy and whites can be drawn into this if they are willing to listen and understand and to argue their point of view with sympathy and commitment and without hostility and prejudice. In what situation do we ever expect everyone to agree on both the ends to pursue and the best means to achieve them? We do not have to agree before we can learn. We have something to learn from trying to understand the various responses of black people, something to gain by supporting them and everything to lose by opposing them.

Appendix

Policies for containment:
the race relations industry

What about the Race Relations Act and the Community Relations Commission – what evidence do they offer that successive governments have taken positive steps to welcome and help the coloured community?

Certainly the existence of the Race Relations Board and the Community Relations Commission is very important. They give the impression that 'something is being done'. But just what is being done?

The 1965 Race Relations Act was introduced to anticipate liberal criticisms of the further restrictions to be introduced later that year. The main provision was to outlaw racial discrimination in 'places of public resort', such as public houses, cinemas and hotels. But the most serious forms of discrimination were experienced in employment, housing and services (insurance, mortgages and loans, car hire etc.); and none of these was covered by the Act. In 1967 a report was published showing the extent of discrimination in these three fields, and a new Act was introduced in 1968.

Race relations legislation is not designed to compel people to love one another. Its sole purpose is to ensure that groups cannot be treated unfairly. In other words you can hate a certain group of people but providing you don't actually incite others to violence against them or deprive them of their rights as citizens or otherwise harm them, you can go on hating them.

Normally such laws do not operate by hauling discriminators before the courts – this is thought to worsen conflict. In the first instance conciliation is sought. If this is refused, then the case may go to court. In 1966 in New York, for example, 287 out of 368 cases were settled by conciliation and a further 30 were settled before or during a court hearing. The situation is thus weighted in favour of the discriminator, as he can avoid further legal action at any time; there is also a tendency to get 'soft settlements' in which there is a compromise rather than an outright admission of the fact of discrimination and a promise to cease.

A good Race Relations Act must cover all situations, work quickly and offer adequate redress. This means that a conciliation officer must have powers immediately to stop discrimination once it looks as if it is taking place. Without such a provision a house might be sold or a job filled before discrimination is finally proved – thus making complaint pointless. Secondly the officer must be able to subpoena witnesses and documents during his investigation; otherwise discriminators might conceal vital documents or just refuse to co-operate with the investigation. To be fully effective also investigators must be able to make enquiries without first receiving a complaint. But in fact the conciliation officers (the men in the field) have no powers of subpoena; they may not institute what the Americans call a 'stop' procedure.

The power to initiate enquiries, which the Race Relations Board has been slow to use, is very important because black people do not always realise the extent to which they are being discriminated against. They may compare experiences with one another but not with a white man. They may seek jobs in a way that does not expose them to discrimination – in fact the more skilled black workers who put themselves into direct competition with white workers are much more aware of discrimination than others.

The statutory provisions of the Race Relations Act do not extend to those parts of industry which have established their own voluntary procedures. Here is an example given by an officer of the RRB who resigned from the Board:

The National Health Service machinery, which has dealt with more cases than any other, has never found discrimination. Nor is it hard to see why, when one looks at the complaint made by Mrs Wint against the Derbyshire Children's Hospital. She alleged that the matron who interviewed her for a nurse's job made denigrating remarks about black nurses and then tore up her application form. The matron agreed that this happened, but the NHS industry machinery formed the opinion that discrimination had not occurred: they spoke of an 'unfortunate misunderstanding', and told the complainant that the fact that she had complained would not prejudice her chances of getting the job if she applied again.

The Race Relations Board operates very slowly, sometimes taking two years with a case. It is not always able to get unequivocal assurances that the person complained against will stop discriminating. Such people are often unco-operative and refuse to meet the Board's officers. Financial settlements are usually pathetically small, if the Board bothers to seek settlements at all.

In the four cases that the Race Relations Board has taken as far as the House of Lords, the Lords have found against them in three cases. The most recent example was the case of the Dockers' Labour Club and Institute of Preston. This club operates a colour bar on membership and refused to serve an associate member from another club, on the grounds of colour. The lower courts held that as the associates of the Clubs and Institutes Union numbered about one million people the clubs could be said to provide a service to the public. Anyone who knows the role of the working man's club will know that it is a key organisation in the working-class community. It would seem fanciful to treat them as private clubs in the strict sense. But the House of Lords did treat them so. In the opinion of Lord Reid the question of the million associates was 'too theoretical to be of any importance'.

The Lord's decision was not forced upon them by the law – they chose to interpret the law in this way. And perhaps we should not be surprised at their decisions. Far more surprising perhaps is that it was the Dockers' Labour Club that wanted to exercise a colour bar. The trade union movement publicly abhors racial discrimination, but does little about it. In this case, for example, it would have been possible to instruct workers engaged in supplying the club with goods and services to have 'blacked' it. But there has not been a murmur of protest, and this is the worst aspect of the whole case.

The Board is usually very deferential to discriminators, especially when they are big companies, government departments or local authorities. But it gives little help to the unaided complainant and often fails fully to inform him of his rights. It is not surprising, therefore, that members of the black population are turning to the Race Relations Board less and less for redress.

Is it possible to take the Race Relations Board seriously when racial discrimination is written into our immigration law and black people regarded in the way they are? If we were a nation with a long history of domestic discrimination, which we were now firmly committed to eliminating, then there would clearly be a case for a board. That case is not so clear in present circumstances. The Board is merely a buffer between discriminator (including the government) and victim, which does nothing to extend the victim's real rights.

The Community Relations Commission presents a picture somewhat similar to the Race Relations Board. The Commission is trying to help black immigrants 'integrate' into British society in a situation of extreme racial conflict which seems to involve the rejection of the black population by the British. The Commission this tries to reconcile interests that are irreconcilable and this often means that it is unable to take any action at all. If for example a local CRC contains members of the main political parties, local authority representatives and representatives of the police, what is it to do to expand the rights and promote the so-called integration of the black community? These groups are all, to a greater or lesser extent, hostile to the local black population. In the early days of the

CRC it was sometimes possible to get *selected* members of the black community to serve on committees. These people were selected by the white members, were usually long established professional or middle-class people or leaders of 'safe' immigrant organisations. But usually the local white notables reserved the right to say who was a leader and what was safe.

Even when the local committes were not weighted against the black community they usually proved ineffective. This was because they defined their role largely in terms of smoothing the passage of black people into a basically united and friendly society. They tried to avoid trouble at all costs. But avoiding trouble in the situation we have described actually means not standing up for the rights of the black community in the face of discrimination by the local authority, not exposing and resisting harassment by the police and not fighting discrimination locally. At the best such organisations pursued paternal policies, telling the black community what was best for it and asserting that most conflict was due either to misunderstanding or the newness of the black people. In achieving compromises between the interests of the local communities the community relations organisations found themselves upholding the status quo.

In due course immigrant communities in many areas became impatient with being told what was good for them. This led to a shift from token representation towards greater representation whereby the immigrants tried to gain influence or control through their own organisations acting on the CRC set-up. This upset the rather cosy and compromised nature of existing organisations and led to cries of 'Black power' and 'Black agitators'. The CRCs even tried to tell the black communities that their own leaders were not genuine.

Not all CRCs took this kind of line. Newcastle-upon-Tyne, for example, appointed a young community relations officer who commanded considerable support among the black communities. His approach was one of defending and expanding the rights of the black communities and of exposing and opposing racism wherever he found it. His reward was to face continual criticism and denial of funds from the Commission and a number of attempts to remove him and to malign him in the eyes of the local authority.

While enduring five years of misery at the hands of the Commission he built up the trust of the people he was hoping to serve and won the respect of all those who tried to understand his work. In his view many local community relations organisations enter into a sort of pact with the local powers-that-be: 'Keep off us, play cool, don't attack commercial, industrial and political authority, don't upset the *status quo*, and we'll see you all right.' The ability to 'see all right' is based upon the local authorities' financial power and their ability to decide the membership of the executive committees of the local community relations committees.

The experience of many other community relations officers has been the same. But not all. There are some whites who seem to be trying to work off their guilt by good works in community relations – they go along with the 'social work' rather than 'community' approach, helping individuals in need but avoiding 'political' action on behalf of the black community. There are also some black people who see the way out of job discrimination and into a respectable career in becoming a CRO.

According to the ex-Tyneside CRO, 'there has been something of a trend towards appointing elderly ex-policemen, ex-ministers, ex-youth workers and ex-civil servants and local government officials as CROs and to senior Commission posts.' Certainly at the local level it is possible to detect a trend towards the increasing of police influence in the executives of CRCs.

Of course there are exceptions to this: CRCs that have black officials and a strong anti-racist line that have been able to resist attempts to suborn their activities.

The value of the CRC is not just questioned at the local level. Here are some of the comments of a senior administrative officer of the Commission who resigned in 1969: 'The real explanation of the Commission's failure is simply that it has not so far managed to equip itself with administrative machinery capable of discharging its functions with tolerable efficiency.' Also: 'Failure to keep staff informed on matters to which they are supposed to be professionally responsible . . . little or no effort to associate them with the way in which decisions are made . . . no clear direction in the allocation of tasks and priorities . . . far too little delegation of authority . . . a disagreeable atmosphere, infecting not only personal relations within the office, but also the conduct of business with other organisations.'

The CRC has been unable at times even to produce leaflets and posters. In 1968 it refused to print an information booklet for immigrants, saying that it was producing one of its own – which did not appear before 1970. At that time in the printing of newsletters, leaflets and booklets it was surpassed by the Quakers. The CRC has actually managed to return unspent money to the government at the end of the year. And when fundamental issues are really at stake – as over the 1968 Immigration Bill – the government is not interested in the National Council for Commonwealth Immigrants, the CRC, or its advice.

In a way the whole concept of 'community relations' is misleading. It is based on a theory that once we have dealt with the problem of immigration (by stopping it) it is only a problem of helping strangers to understand our ways, our language and customs and to understand one another. The implementation of the immigration colour bar (which is seldom discussed) makes nonsense of the ideas of social harmony that the local dignitaries and others on CRCs try to adopt. The 'problem' is one of the systematic and deliberate domination and exploitation of a mass of immigrants – who occupy a special position within British society and the British economy. They are not separate communities in this sense. Nor do they need integrating – they are already integrated: into the lowest-paid and worst-unionised jobs, in the service and high-risk sectors of the economy, in menial and unpleasant tasks that are needed to keep our affluence enjoyable. They are fully integrated *at the bottom*. The question is do we organise to keep them at the bottom, or do we organise for something else ? When you ask this question the problem of 'community relations' pales a little. Clearly where the CRCs have been taken over by organised immigrant groups, they are challenging their lowly status and asserting the right to decide their own future. And here we hear the frightened cry of 'Black power' or 'Black militants' from worried whites who feel that their scheme of things for the black population is about to be overturned.

Perhaps none of this would matter because as Wilfred Wood (a clergyman prominent in black affairs) once said, 'if the CRC was to fold up today, not one black man would notice the difference.' Nor would anybody else.

But in fact the CRC is important. Its very setting up created political difficulties for the immigrant communities. The old NCCI and the CRC both posed a problem for the immigrants: perhaps the organisations set up were confidence tricks, but should they nonetheless use whatever channels were opened for them to the authorities ? If they ignored the set-up they would be branded as ungrateful, unco-operative and unwilling to use the supposed best means open to them. The decision whether to collaborate with the NCCI split immigrant organisations and also deeply divided and hastened the destruction of an emerging civil rights organisation. 'Merely by coming into existence the NCCI had delivered one of its most damaging blows to the embryo civil rights movement,' was how Michael Dummett put it. His wife was later to resign as Oxford CRO.

Then, of course, immigrant leaders who stayed outside the NCCI/CRC organisation were dubbed 'unrepresentative', because in the eyes of the authorities representative people collaborated with them and the others were troublemakers. A similar distinction is made between 'moderate' or 'reasonable' trade union officials and shop floor 'agitators'.

Setting up both the CRC and the RRB has created 'official

channels' for dealing with immigrants' grievances. The fact that these are bad – at times even hostile or unhelpful – channels is irrelevant. People in Britain who don't use the proper channels deserve what they get – and they certainly get no sympathy from those members of the public who know very little but who believe that everything is being done to 'these people' through the CCR and RRB.

What the CRC and RRB have done is to create *controlled* (white authority-controlled) channels for the immigrant; in so doing they have rendered any other activity by immigrants in pursuit of justice or any other rights illegitimate. The British are great believers in 'proper channels', just as they are opponents of 'unofficial' action.

These proper channels also get the responsible politicians off the hook. They are insulated from the consequences of their own acts. They adopt anti-black policies and then expect the RRB, or more likely the CRC, to clear up the mess and quieten things down again. British political parties and political activities are based on the conflict of social classes within an industrial society, and all our political institutions reflect this. 'Race' is outside this set-up, and confuses the issues for politicians and trade union officials. So they have 'subcontracted' the race question to specialist organisations while they get on with what they regard as the *real* business of politics. Unfortunately for them both the extreme right and the black community think otherwise and regard the question of race as rather central to a number of political matters.

If the RRB was really effective in fighting discrimination and the CRC actively fought for the rights of the immigrant population, it would still mean that the black population was denied direct access to the political process. They would have to go through the extra stage of taking their issues through the Board and the Commission and having them mediated by them to Parliament. This would not be the black community discovering its own solutions to its own problems and developing its political muscle through its own action. It would prevent precisely the kind of development which surrounded the Imperial Typewriters strike and the Kenilworth dispute.

In fact at both the national and local level the RRB and its conciliation committees and the CRC and local organisations act as a buffer between the black population and the white authorities. In a way this is what they are meant to be. Perhaps they are curiously appropriate as a system of indirect rule – something quite familiar to the inhabitants of a colony.

Sections of the white community are quite right to be worried by the power struggles that go on within and around local CRCs: these struggles are important aspects of black mobilisation and can be seen as attempts to take control of the organisations designed to control them and to contain their political power.

The Uganda Resettlement Board is the most recent example in which the government appeared to be trying to do some good for the black population in Britain. When General Amin expelled the Asians from Uganda, the British government set up a Resettlement Board to aid the British refugees arriving in the United Kingdom. From the end of August 1972 until the end of March 1973, 28,165 Ugandan Asians passed through the arrangements made by the Board, 21,797 of these coming into the special resettlement centres which it set up, mainly in military camps.

Such an operation sounds like a major effort by the government to meet the immediate personal needs of a section of the coloured British population. A great deal of personal help was given by an army of volunteer workers and many voluntary organisations, without whom the Board reported it could not have operated. But the crucial question is how it interpreted its role in a wider sense. In practice, the Board received citizens into centres where accommodation was provided and information collected from local authorities and others offering help. The citizen-refugees were moved out of the centres, at which point they became the responsibility of the local authority which was receiving them. The Board gave aid to the authorities for one year only. No direct help was given to the citizens once they had left the centres, and they were not allowed to return once they had left.

The Board declared some areas to be 'red' areas in which social resources were under such great pressure that they could not receive any refugees. No aid was given to those intending to go to red areas. In fact these areas were those that did not want Asians and had said so; the High Commission in Uganda had advertised to tell Asians not to go to certain areas in Britain, and Leicester had gone so far as to advertise in Uganda to tell Asians not to come to their city. An enquiry later shows that some red areas were better off for housing and employment than the so-called green areas. What was happening was that the Board was trying to operate a policy of dispersal in respect to racist pressures from particular areas.

In August 1973 a survey of Asians in one red area showed that a quarter of breadwinners were unemployed, three-quarters unsatisfactorily housed. Those paying high rents were badly hit by the wage stop. A survey of four London boroughs – all red areas – shows that three-quarters were unsettled. These surveys underline the shortsightedness of not providing the Asians with a resettlement after-care, particularly when they were almost certain to go to some areas of great racial hostility in order to join friends and relatives. The Resettlement Board looked more like a reception and dispersal board and not an agency dedicated to solving settlement problems, which are long-term problems. In March 1973, 3,380 people were still in resettlement centres; many of these had relatives separated from them. For example, out of 171 men over 18 years of age in a Belgian refugee camp, 78 had family ties with Britain. These men could not of course, discuss arrangements with their families who were in Britain. Husbands of families in Britain were eventually let in later in the year.

A report by the Co-ordinating Committee for the Welfare of Evacuees from Uganda published on 26 September 1973, stated that three-quarters of those coming from Uganda had received no permanent settlement help from the government through the Board. The government saw its responsibility as terminating when 'the Asian families take their rightful place in the poverty line'. According to the chairman of the Executive Committee of the Co-ordinating Committee (a member of the Resettlement Board), 'the vast majority who came to this country did not join the general population; they joined the homeless, the unemployed and the socially-deprived.'

What lessons can be learnt from all this? One thing is quite clear, we will not quickly reverse the policies that have led to the immigration colour bar. Both major parties are committed to this bar, whatever they might say about it. It is much more likely that when majority rule is established in Zimbabwe (Rhodesia), many of the whites – who have been described as 'Enoch Powell's lost voters' – will be free to return to the United Kingdom. As most of them went out after the war to enjoy the benefits of white supremacy, they will return filled with the greatest possible race hatred and sense of resentment.

This points to one major factor in the whole discussion of 'race relations'. Many of the most important activities likely to bring about changes for us will take place overseas, largely beyond our control. Many more embargoes could be adopted against Europe – perhaps to ensure that we treat black populations at home and abroad more justly. The outcome of such contests is by no means clear, because the rich are very rich and powerful and the poor very poor. But at least we can see that new questions may be raised in talking about future relations between races and nations. Thus questions relating to the 'Third World' and poverty overseas are not as remote from the man on the shop floor or the housewife as they may seem. But they are not questions that can be solved by holding flag days and jumble sales. They are problems rooted in the very nature of the economic system in which we live and which create the everyday problems that are familiar to ordinary people at work and in the supermarket.

The RRB and CRC do not impinge very much on the life

of the average black, nor does the white housewife or shop-floor worker feel their presence. The cause of the black citizen will not be advanced by setting up committees with official backing. None of the ways in which black people fight back against oppression and exploitation involves making formal approaches to official committees. The fight back is in their own hands.